How to Write a Résumé and Get a Job

Other Books in the Esperanza Series
(also available in Spanish)

How to Buy a House

There Is an Answer: How to Prevent and
Understand HIV/AIDS

A Simple Guide to U.S. Immigration and Citizenship

How to Fix Your Credit

Esperanza Series

How to Write a Résumé and Get a Job

Reverend Luis Cortés Jr.

with Karin Price Mueller

ATRIA BOOKS

NEW YORK LONDON TORONTO SYDNEY

ATRIA BOOKS

A Division of Simon & Schuster, Inc.
1230 Avenue of the Americas
New York, NY 10020

First Atria Books trade paperback edition May 2007

ATRIA BOOKS and colophon are trademarks
of Simon & Schuster, Inc.

For information about special discounts for bulk purchases,
please contact Simon & Schuster Special Sales:
1-800-456-6798 or business@simonandschuster.com.

Manufactured in the United States of America

1   3   5   7   9   10   8   6   4   2

Library of Congress Cataloging-in-Publication Data

Cortés, Luis, Reverend.
How to write a résumé and get a job / Luis Cortés, Jr. with Karin Price Mueller.
p. cm.
1. Résumés (Employment).
I. Mueller, Karin Price, 1970– . II. Title.
HF5383.C657 2007
650.14'2—dc22   200706050

ISBN-13: 978-0-7432-8792-0
ISBN-10:   0-7432-8792-4

Acknowledgments

As always, there are many to thank. First, Karin Price Mueller, who has become a great partner on this project. To Arlene Cruz-Larsen for her administrative assistance, and Priscilla Rodriquez, Tanya Bird, and Nelidia Sepulveda, who are practitioners at Esperanza and have assisted many people find their first or next job. My family, as usual, steps aside and lets me do my thing; thank you all. To the good people at Atria who are always patient with my product, thank you. Special thanks to Johanna Castillo and Amy Tannenbaum for their assistance and encouragement.

Contents

- *Mentally Prepare*
    RESEARCH · PRACTICE INTERVIEW QUESTIONS · LEGAL
    AND ILLEGAL INTERVIEW QUESTIONS · BE CALM

- *What to Bring*

- *A Good First Impression*

- *Interview Tests*

- *Follow Up with a Note*

CHAPTER 7
Securing Your Victory   68

- *Questions to Ask*
    THE SALARY · A DOLLAR FIGURE · HOW MUCH DO YOU
    WANT TO BE PAID? · NEGOTIATE FOR BENEFITS · NOT
    ACCEPTING A JOB · HEALTH AND DENTAL INSURANCE ·
    RETIREMENT BENEFITS · PAID PERSONAL DAYS, SICK
    DAYS, VACATION DAYS, AND HOLIDAYS · DAY CARE
    ASSISTANCE · PERFORMANCE REVIEWS AND RAISES ·
    HOW OFTEN WILL I BE PAID? · WHAT ARE ALL YOUR
    BENEFITS WORTH?

- *Your First Day on the Job*
    TAX PAPERWORK · WORKING IN THE UNITED STATES ·
    DIRECT DEPOSIT · LIFE INSURANCE BENEFITS ·
    HEALTH INSURANCE BENEFITS · RETIREMENT BENEFITS

- *Enjoy Your Success*

Introduction

You're ready! You're ready to search for a new job. It's taken some energy and some courage to decide to pick up this book and start taking steps to find the employment you need.

The process of finding a job does not have to be complicated, but it demands two things from you from start to finish: consistency and perseverance. Consistency involves making sure you're as prepared as you can be to give 100 percent to the effort of finding a job. Perseverance requires you to understand that there is a job out there for you, but that you may not find it right away. You may have to exhaust yourself to find the right job, but it's well worth it. If you apply consistency and perseverance to your search, you will increase your chances of finding or bettering your employment.

Reading this book is a smart start to your job search, and no matter how difficult the task ahead, this book is intended to help you every step of the way. After following the steps in this book, you will be in a better position to find employment than when you began.

I want you to consider, however, that while employment is one of the most important things that you can do with your time, it should not define you. Who we are is more important than what we do. We must understand that we are all created in the image of God. We are beings with the ability to create, to change, and to enhance not only ourselves but the environment around us. Genesis, the first book of the Bible, states that God created the world in six days, and on the seventh, he rested. To be created in the image of God is to understand that we, too, are called to create with our labor, and that we are then to rest and remember who created us.

We all have a vocation, a mission at which God wants us to excel. You should understand that your job may not be your vocation. Our job may be what we do for subsistence, to earn money, but not what we do for our mission or creativity. For example, Jesus Christ was a carpenter, yet we do not remember him as much for his job as a carpenter as we do for his vocation, which was his mission to minister.

Work gives us fulfillment. God designed our world with the concept that work should allow us to explore and experience life. In Genesis, God tells us that we are to labor for our livelihood: "We would eat and survive by the sweat of our brow." Work is a responsibility and we should approach it with confidence, dignity, and the sense that we are reflecting the image of God.

Knowing this, we are required to perform to our highest ability. We should bring honor to God with our performance and show others that we are worthy of the opportunity we have. Often, today's society makes the mistake of judging people by their financial income. In the Bible, Christ answered the tempter, "Man does not live by bread alone." We are not to be measured only in dollars. God measures us by the service we provide to others, whether we are loving our neighbors, feeding the hungry, clothing the sick, visiting the imprisoned or the infirm. It is by our service to our fellow human beings that we are measured, not by our weekly paycheck.

Wealth is a means to serve others, yet we live in a society where this is rarely done. Do not become fixated on making more and more money, accumulating more and more wealth, if it's at the cost of losing the opportunity to help others. The boundaries of too much wealth and its investment are a question of meditation and study that I believe is a part of your spiritual development. The question of vocation and mission are part of this book's agenda to show you that your job and vocation can be the same.

When searching for work, it's important to be in the right frame of mind. I recommend that you begin your job search by meditating on what God would like for you. Is there a particular vocation or calling that is deep in your consciousness? Do you have a missional purpose to serve others in need? Those are special callings and require much reflection and to some extent the support and guidance of people in the service field. Regardless of your calling, this book will help you move in the right direction.

Do not fall for the idea that any work is good. Not all work is ethical. Only ethical work is an acceptable way of earning a living according to the law *and* according to your conscience. There are jobs that are legal, but your conscience may tell you that they are wrong. If your conscience alerts you that something is wrong, listen to it! Do not take a job that contradicts what your conscience tells you. One example would be the pornography industry. While many aspects of the industry are legal and protected by the laws of the United States, it is ultimately an industry that demeans women and abuses God's intention for sexuality. While a job in this industry is legal, it is neither vocational nor missional, and, in all likelihood, should be avoided.

Work is "the expenditure of energy (manual, mental or both) in the service of others, which brings fulfillment to the worker, benefit to the community and glory to God."* This is an important definition for workers to understand, especially for those who may feel underappreciated or less esteemed in their work setting. For example, cleaning an office is the custodian's way of expending his or her energy in the service of others. If done with pride and diligence, it brings fulfillment to the custodian and clear benefit to the community. In an employee's pursuit of excellence at work and his or her positive use of the income earned for their labor, God is glorified. These connections can uplift us, even if others view our work tasks as insignificant or unimportant.

You are made in the image of God. Regardless of how long it may take you, consistency and perseverance will find you a job. God is with us, so let's not fret. Turn the page and take your first step toward finding a job.

* John Stott, *Issues Facing Christians Today,* 3rd ed. (Grand Rapids, Mich.: Zondervan, 1999), p. 163.

How to Write a Résumé and Get a Job

CHAPTER 1

What a Job Can Do for You

A job isn't everything. But it can give you what you need to make your life more pleasurable, more comfortable, more satisfying. To wake up every morning and have a mission.

That mission, whether you're employed as an office worker, a garbage collector, a waitress, or a computer technician, should take you closer to reaching your life's goals.

Work, and a paycheck, will allow you to provide financially for yourself and your loved ones. You'll earn money that will put food on your table and clothing on your children's backs. You may receive benefits from your job, such as health care insurance, which will enable you to take better care of your family's physical well-being. You'll have the chance to set money aside for future goals, such as buying your own home or sending your children to college. It's the key to a better future.

But a job isn't just about a paycheck or receiving a salary. It's about self-respect and emotional growth. Being an employed member of society gives you an opportunity that the unemployed don't have. You'll be respected as a responsible member of society who can contribute to the community through the job you perform each day.

A job is a fantastic learning experience. Your work might teach you new skills that can open you to new opportunities. Of course, you'll learn how to perform the duties required for your job, but you can take it further and learn more. You can see how a company or business operates. You may be exposed to other jobs you're interested in trying.

Along the way, you'll meet people who will observe the work you do, and depending on how well you perform, they may choose to help you take the next step. You may even learn skills that will enable you to start your own business, if that's your goal.

Whatever job you choose, it is important to take pride in the work you do. Your attitude will be reflected in how well you're able to perform on the job and will define you as an employee with a future.

Establish Your Job Goals

Not every job is right for every person. Before you start your search, you need to decide what kind of a job you want and what kind of a job you're qualified for.

Perhaps you've always wanted to be a clothing buyer for a department store, someone who chooses the latest fashions that will be sold in shops, but you've never worked in the clothing industry. Without experience, you can't simply walk into a store and say you want to be their buyer. If you apply for a position as a clothing buyer, you're probably going to be rejected, not because you're not capable but because you are unable to verify that you can do the job. You don't have the right kind of experience.

Your first step is to be realistic about your skills and your experience, and to apply for jobs for which you're qualified. Realistic goals will lead you to success.

That doesn't mean that you can't better yourself to work your way up to the top. Just don't expect to start there. Many heads of companies began at the bottom and learned while they worked. Many restaurant owners started out as busboys or waitresses. Newspaper publishers started as paperboys or pressmen. And clothing buyers started as salespeople.

When you're trying to decide what kind of job to search for, you first need to consider the following:

❑ **What makes you happy?** If you don't like animals, you shouldn't seek work at a veterinary office. If you aren't comfortable making conversation with strangers, customer service or telemarketing may not be for you. But if you love children, you might consider working at a day care center. If you have a fondness for fine food, a gourmet restaurant may be a perfect fit. You may be qualified for many jobs you won't enjoy, but if you can find a workplace that will pay you to do something you love, you'll be happier in your job and you'll be a better employee.

❑ **When do you need to work?** Some jobs are very steady, starting at 9 a.m. and ending at 5 p.m. Other jobs require that you work weekends or at night, and those varying hours may not fit into your lifestyle. If you have school-age children, you may be willing to work only when they're at school. If that's the case, working in a hospital, where patients need care all day and all night, may not be for you. If you don't have children, or if you have a partner or other family members willing to care for your children, you may not need to be home at night. Off-hour jobs could fit nicely into your lifestyle.

❑ **What kind of atmosphere do you like?** Different jobs require different levels of professionalism, and even seriousness. Retail jobs in busy stores with a high volume of customers will allow you to meet many new people. Being friendly and having an outgoing personality would be an asset in a place like this. Or if you pursue an office job, you may have to sit at a desk all day long in front of a computer screen without many people to talk to. Some jobs require business suits, while others welcome casual dress. You should choose a job with an environment that suits you.

❑ **What do you want for the future?** Forget the past. Don't say "what if?" What if you hadn't dropped out of school? What if you had taken that job ten years ago? What if you had waited longer before having a child? The past is the past, and looking back isn't what matters now. It's looking ahead to your future and where you want to go that's important. Even if you have little or no experience in the working world, you have many valuable skills. You can use those skills to find your next job, which may put you on the path to a long-term career. You might start out in an entry-level position and work your way up to more prestigious, higher-level work. If there's a higher-level job you want, consider starting out with a job that will help you learn the skills that you'll need to move to the next level.

Most important, remember that you don't have to stay in any job forever. If you don't like the job or the industry you've chosen, you're not stuck there. Most people change careers several times during their lives. If the job you've taken isn't working out, you can always look for something else that better fits your interests, your wants, and your abilities. We'll talk more about how to choose the best job for you in chapter 3.

What Am I Willing to Do for a Job?

Every job commands respect. Even jobs you might consider unappealing provide an important service for someone, or for something, in society. Think of some of the jobs people aren't quite dreaming about, such as working in your city's sanitation department. Your first impression might be that it's a dirty, distasteful job, but there are great benefits. Many city jobs offer pension plans (which will pay you money when you've retired after working for a certain number of years), and they often offer other benefits, such as health care and life insurance. And these workers perform an essential service. They keep our streets clean and they keep our garbage out of neighborhoods. Without them, life would be very unpleasant indeed.

To think that a food service or a construction job is not up to your level has little to do with the job itself. It's more about how you're looking at the job. Many waitresses and construction workers have advanced their positions and are now restaurant owners or established builders. If you choose to make this your goal, you can take any job and turn it into an opportunity for advancement.

So while you may have job preferences, you should try to feel that nothing is beneath you. Few people are so talented or irreplaceable that they don't have to make some concessions when they take on a new job. What's most important about a job is different for every individual. You need to set your own priorities so you can search for a position that offers you much of what you want, without forcing you to endure too many hardships or give up too much. Some considerations:

❏ How much money do you need to earn to support yourself and possibly your family? We all want a big paycheck, but what is the minimum you need to cover your bills?
❏ Do you need a job that offers health insurance? Perhaps you'd forgo a higher salary in exchange for this benefit.
❏ Are you only willing and available to work certain hours?
❏ Are you willing to travel for a job?
❏ Are there any jobs that you morally oppose? For example, perhaps you have had bad experiences with the effects of alcohol in the past, or someone close to you died in a drunk driving accident, or your religious convictions would dictate that working in a bar or liquor store would be a poor fit.
❏ Do you want to break into a certain industry? If you know what your dream job is, would you take a lower position in that industry to get on that track?

Create a list for yourself so that as you search for work, you can keep these priorities in the forefront of your mind. Here is an example:

What Must This Job Have?	What Do I Want?	What Don't I Want?
salary of $25,000 a year daytime hours	health insurance benefits retirement benefits	work with pets night/weekend hours a desk job

When you read help wanted ads or consider applying for certain positions, you can refer to your list to make sure that the job you're considering will provide the essentials of what you need, hopefully some of what you want, and none of what you don't want.

Whether you're unhappy with the job you have now, or you're ready to embark on a new adventure by joining the working world, you can get a position that's right for you and your lifestyle.

Let's explore how you can learn what kinds of opportunities are out there waiting and how you can find them.

CHAPTER 2

Know Your Market

When you go shopping for chicken, you don't look in a hair salon. If you need toothpaste, you don't go to a video rental store. You'd be wasting your time.

You should treat your job search similarly. It wouldn't be efficient to blindly start calling stores, businesses, or other potential employers to ask if they'll hire you. To save yourself a lot of time and effort, you should first do some research.

Today's Job Market

All areas of business need employees. Gas stations and public relations firms and shoe stores must have workers to keep things running. But there are certain industries that are growing very fast today, and they need to fill specific jobs. That could mean opportunity for you.

According to the Bureau of Labor Statistics (BLS), the government agency that tracks job-related statistics in the United States, some occupations are expected to be the most needed in the next five years. Some of the biggest growth is expected to be in the health care industry. The so-called baby boomer generation (the large group of people born in the decade or so after World War II) is getting older. They're needing, or they're expected to need, more health care and elder care services, such as home health aids, medical assistants, physician assistants, medical records and information technicians, and physical therapists.

Child care is also an expanding trade in this country. More families have both parents working, or only a single parent who works, and there's a rising number of families that have young children. The BLS expects child care services to grow 43 percent by 2012.

For more information on the hottest industries today, and what kinds of skills and education these jobs require, check out the Department of Labor's Career Voyages Web site (www.careervoyages. gov) or look at the link on the Esperanza USA site (www.esperanza.us).

Where to Start Looking

Though it's possible, it's unlikely that a job is going to find you. You have to look. There are many ways to find employment, and here are some of the places you can search:

THE INTERNET

You can find literally thousands of job ads posted on the Internet.

Even if you don't have a computer, you can get access to one. Your family or friends, your local library, even your child's school may give you access to their computers. This is a very important part of your job search.

Online, the Department of Labor (DOL) sponsors Career One-Stop, which can direct you to a One-Stop location near you where you'll find job counselors who can give you assistance with your résumé and other free services (www.careeronestop.org). You can also call 1-877-US-2JOBS for information.

Many job Web sites allow you to search in particular fields, for certain job titles, and by geographic area. They also offer information on the company that's looking to hire so you can do all of your research in one stop. You may also be able to apply online either by e-mailing your résumé or through the company's Web site.

Many online job-posting sites offer a valuable résumé-posting service, too. Instead of just looking through dozens, even hundreds of ads, you can post your résumé on the site. Employers looking to hire will go to the site's database of résumés and search for people who fit their job requirements.

Additionally, these sites often have e-mail services that allow you to sign up to be notified of jobs that meet your criteria.

There are hundreds of Web sites for jobs. Some are very broad, listing jobs in fields from restaurants and retailing to rocket science and nanotechnology. Some sites are far better than others, and some even list only jobs in particular industries. If you were looking for a job in the publishing field, you might want to check www.Media Bistro.com or www.JournalismJobs.com. Others are regional in nature. Look around to see which sites cover the types of positions you're interested in.

Here's a list of some of the most popular and largest job-posting Web sites. (You can also find these links at www.esperanza.us.)

- ❏ Monster (www.monster.com): This is one of the biggest and most popular job search sites. You can post your résumé and search for jobs.
- ❏ Career Builder (www.careerbuilder.com): This site posts newspaper help wanted ad listings.
- ❏ America's Job Bank (www.americasjobbank.com): This site offers links to state employment and career service Web sites. You can also post your résumé online.
- ❏ Hot Jobs (www.hotjobs.com): You can post your résumé or search for jobs by industry, location, and company.
- ❏ Your local newspaper: Most newspapers offer their classified ads on their own Web sites.

Some of these sites require you to register before you can search or post your résumé. Many also offer memberships for varying fees, or have different levels of membership, some free, some not. You don't need to pay for job listings, so opt for the free membership.

When you register, make sure you don't give out any private information, such as your Social Security number. Legitimate sites won't ask for that kind of information.

Finally, one note on confidentiality: If you only have an e-mail address from your current employer, you shouldn't use it when searching for a job. Sign up for a free e-mail address on sites such as Yahoo!, AOL, or MSN Hotmail. This way you don't take advantage of your current employer, or risk that he will see you're getting job-posting e-mails.

CLASSIFIED ADS

Classified ads, also called help wanted ads, are found in local newspapers. You can find jobs of all kinds in the classified ad section of a newspaper. The Sunday paper usually has the largest help wanted section, and some papers also offer a special section during the week devoted to job ads. You can purchase them or use free copies of newspapers at your local library.

Employers like to use these ads because unlike online job listings, the newspaper classifieds tend to target potential employees who live close to the business. If an employer doesn't want to pay relocation costs for an employee, he may prefer to hire locally.

If you're not able to buy the paper every day, remember you can check the newspaper's Web site for daily job postings.

EMPLOYMENT AGENCIES

An employment agency matches job applicants with companies looking to fill jobs. You'll find employment agencies listed in your phone book and online.

These companies don't find jobs for free, so your first question should be who pays their fees—you or the company that's hiring—and how much. Sometimes the company will pay the fee, but depending on your state's laws, the cost could be shared by the employer and the job seeker or you alone could be responsible for paying it. You need to know this outright and before you consider signing on with an employment agency.

The Federal Trade Commission, or FTC (www.ftc.gov), is a U.S. government agency in charge of making sure businesses don't take advantage of consumers. In the case of employment agencies, the FTC needs to make sure that no firm is misrepresenting what it can do for a job seeker or is overcharging for its services.

The FTC offers these warnings about employment agencies on its Web site:

- When you're looking for help in finding a job, it's important to understand the differences among employment services. Many terms, such as *employment agency, personnel placement service, executive search firm,* and *executive counseling service,* are used interchangeably. Find out what services a firm offers, how much the services cost, and who pays. If you're required to pay the fee, find out what you'll owe if the employment service fails to find you a job or any leads.
- Be suspicious of any employment-service firm that promises to get you a job.
- Be skeptical of any employment-service firm that charges up-front fees, even if it guarantees refunds to dissatisfied customers.
- Don't give out your credit card or bank account information on the phone unless you're familiar with the company and agree to pay for something. Anyone who has your account information can use it to commit financial fraud against you.
- Get a copy of the firm's contract and review it carefully before you pay any money. Understand the terms and conditions of the firm's refund policy. Make sure you understand what services will be provided by the firm and what you'll be responsible for. If oral promises are made that don't also appear in the contract, think twice about doing business with the firm.
- Take your time reviewing the contract. Don't be rushed into paying for services. Avoid high-pressure sales pitches that require you to pay now or risk losing out on the opportunity.
- Be cautious about purchasing from a firm that's reluctant to answer your questions or gives you evasive answers.
- Follow up with the offices of any company or organization listed in an ad by an employment service, to find out if the company's really hiring.
- Be wary of firms promoting "previously undisclosed" federal government jobs. All federal positions are announced to the public.

❏ Check with your local consumer protection agency, state Attorney General's Office, and the Better Business Bureau to see if any complaints have been filed about a company with which you intend to do business.

❏ In addition, federal law prohibits the use of a toll-free number for pay-per-call 900-number services. This means that anyone calling a toll-free number cannot be charged simply for completing the call, and that a toll-free number call cannot be transferred, or connected, to a pay-per-call 900-number service. Federal law also prohibits any telephone message that solicits calls to a pay-per-call 900-number service from failing to disclose the cost of the call.

Employment agencies can be a useful tool in a job search, but make sure no one is trying to take advantage of you.

TEMP AGENCIES

Temp agencies help companies fill their needs for temporary employees, such as to cover a maternity leave, sick leave, or other short-term shortage of workers.

Even if you're looking for a permanent position, working with a temp agency can provide a foot in the door. Temping, or working in a temporary job, can help you meet important people at a company you might want to work for full-time. You can get a good feel for what it would be like to work permanently for the company, and it can help you decide if you'd fit in well. You can also take a peek at what kinds of skills you might need, and learn a lot about those skills during your temporary employment.

Like employment agencies, some temp agencies specialize in certain industries, so check your phone book and call around to find an agency that fits your skill set or your interests. You can also sign up with more than one agency, and you may find better pay and better jobs with one over another. When work becomes available, you'll be called and you can choose to take the job or not.

Many temp agencies offer their workers training on everything from computer skills to office etiquette. That alone might make look-ing into a temp agency worth your while.

SCHOOL CAREER CENTERS

If you've attended college, even if you graduated years ago, you can still take advantage of your school's career center. If you're not a col-lege graduate, you still have options. If you sign up for one class as a part-time student, you'll probably have access to the career center and all it has to offer. Or call your high school and see if it has a career cen-ter you can use for your job search. Trade and vocational schools often have career counseling services, too.

Career centers offer everything from job listings to résumé and interview coaching to career counseling. If you get to know the people who work in the career center and they hear about a job that fits your qualifications, they'll think of you and give you a call.

Best of all, these services are free.

CAREER ONE-STOP

As mentioned earlier in this chapter, the U.S. Department of Labor offers Career One-Stop (www.careeronestop.org or call 1-877-US-2JOBS). These offices are open to anyone who needs help finding a job or looking for a new one, and their services are free. Job coun-selors will help you find information on jobs, write your résumé and cover letters, and develop your interview skills.

JOB FAIRS

Job fairs, also called career fairs, can be a wonderland for job seekers. At these organized events, dozens of employers from different types of companies come looking for people just like you.

Come to these events with your updated résumé in hand, and get ready to impress. You can introduce yourself and learn about the com-pany, while the company's recruiters can learn about you and what you have to offer. (We'll talk more about interviewing skills in chapter 6.)

HELP WANTED SIGNS

After all this talk about Internet resources, employment agencies, and job fairs, answering a help wanted sign might sound a little low-tech. It is, but it can still be an effective way of finding a job.

When a company needs to fill a job, it will often put a help wanted sign in the window. As you spend time in your neighborhood, passing stores and businesses, keep your eyes out for them. If you see one, go inside and ask about the job. (If you're not neatly dressed, or if you're carrying bags from a shopping trip or you have your children along, consider coming back when you'll be able to present yourself in the best light, and bring your résumé.)

You may get to see the boss right away, or you might be directed to fill out an application on the spot. Take advantage of the opportunity.

NETWORKING

Networking isn't as complicated as it might sound. It's simply using the people you know to learn about job opportunities. When you're looking for a job, you should tell everyone you know. Your family members, your friends, past employers, friendly clerks you meet in a store—you never know who might know about a job opening that could be right for you.

THE YELLOW PAGES

If you're looking for a specific type of job with a specific company, go directly to the source. Open your phone book to search for companies that fit what you're looking for and call. Ask for the human resources department, or if it's a small company, ask for the owner or the manager. Introduce yourself and explain what you can offer as an employee and see if there's any interest. You can follow up later with a copy of your résumé, or even ask if you can come in to speak to the person in charge of hiring.

What Employers Want

Now you've seen some job postings or ads and you think you'd be interested in some of the positions. But do you have what it takes? Maybe. First, make sure you understand what the employer is looking for.

Generally speaking, employers want dependable employees with experience in the field. If you don't have the right kind of experience for a particular job, it doesn't mean you don't have a chance. You can show an employer your best qualities, and take steps to learn the specific skills he or she wants you to have.

WHAT DOES THIS JOB MEAN?

You may have a good understanding of what an employer wants when the ads says "plumber," "nurse," or "travel agent," but there are plenty of job titles that are a little harder to decipher, especially if you're new to the field. If you don't understand the job you're applying for, you probably won't get a very good response from an employer, and you'll be wasting your time. Instead, make sure you know what you're applying for.

Monster (www.monster.com) offers a great listing of job titles and what they mean, what education or skills are required, and even an outlook for job growth in various industries. You can also find links for related careers.

The Web site Wet Feet offers similar information on jobs, with detailed job descriptions, requirements, salary, and more (www.wetfeet.com/Content/Careers.aspx).

Another resource is Career Journal (www.careerjournal.com), connected to *The Wall Street Journal.* This site is geared toward management and professional jobs, offering job descriptions, salary information, and hiring trends in different industries.

WHAT SKILLS DO I NEED?

Most job ads are quite specific about the skills an employer is looking for in an employee. You may see lines such as:

❏ Proficient in Microsoft Word and Excel.
❏ Bachelor's degree or some college is preferred.
❏ 3+ years general management experience in this industry.
❏ Must have flexibility in hours/days worked.

Employers respond best to job applicants who already have the skills needed for the job, so you should start by targeting jobs that you're already qualified for.

If there's something in an ad you're not sure about, do some research. You can use Internet search engines such as Google or Yahoo! to look for more information about skills listed in an ad. Say, for example, many of the jobs you're interested in require knowledge of Excel. You know this is a computer program, but you're not sure what it's used for. Look it up online, then see if you can find any training courses in your area. Or, when you apply for the job, explain that you don't know Excel but you're a fast learner and if the employer would be willing to train you, he or she wouldn't be disappointed with the results.

Make sure your résumé reflects the specific skill set the employer says they're looking for. That may mean you need a few versions of your résumé if there are several different job types you're applying for. (We'll talk more about how to build and write a great résumé in chapter 4.)

If you don't have any of the skills mentioned in the ad, perhaps it's time to get some training. Or if you're currently taking a class that would help you with a specific job, let that employer know. They may be willing to hire someone who has already taken the initiative to start learning.

GOOD QUALITIES FOR ANY JOB

Whatever your specific experience, there are plenty of qualities that just about every employer wants in their workforce. If you only have some of the skills required for a particular job, you'll have a much better chance if you can impress your future boss with the following:

❏ **Reliability:** When you take a job, you promise your employer that you'll show up for work on time, every time, unless there's a dire emergency. Convince your potential employer that you can be counted on. To make sure you do your part, if you're a heavy sleeper, have two alarm clocks, have a backup babysitter for your kids in case your regular sitter can't make it, or leave for work a little early so you're never held up in traffic.

❑ **Flexibility:** Workers who are willing to accept new challenges and changing situations in the workplace are extremely valuable. Too often, employers face workers who are stuck in their "old ways." Show that you can be flexible, open-minded, and accommodating.

❑ **Energy:** No one wants to see a worker who's tired and lethargic on the job, or completely unexcited to be there. They want to see people ready to face the day's work with enthusiasm. Show up with a smile on your face and be ready for whatever the day may bring.

❑ **Communication skills:** Nothing makes a workplace run more smoothly than communication. Whether there's a problem with a customer or with a coworker, or if you have some ideas on how to improve something at work, speaking your mind, with respect, can thrill a boss. Employers need to know what's going on in their businesses, and they count on their employees to communicate with them about important items. You'll please your boss by being open, honest, and forthcoming with information. Show any prospective boss good communication skills and you'll increase your chance of getting hired. Showing that you can communicate well in more than one language is another big asset.

❑ **Confidence:** It can be hard to work with meek, shy people. You can't tell what the person is thinking, and if they're really quiet, it can be hard to tell if they're doing their job well. In contrast, a worker who displays confidence will inspire others. Confident people learn how to get things done.

❑ **You're a problem solver:** Sometimes problems at work don't have an easy or obvious solution. You need to be creative, imaginative, and resourceful. You have to be willing to try new ideas to come up with an answer. Tell your future employer that you know how to solve problems, and give them an example of one of your successes.

Do Some Research

Before you apply for a job, you should know a little something about a company. It will help you decide if it's a company you'd like to work for. Sure, a secretary at a publishing company may do a lot of the same tasks as a secretary for a trucking company, but you might find one company more interesting than the other.

Learning about the company you'd like to work for will give you an advantage when you meet your future employer. You'll be able to show that you know a little something about the business, even if you've never held a position in the industry before.

Many of the job Web sites give you the option to learn more about the company posting the job, but one of the most comprehensive sites if you want to learn about a company is ZoomInfo (www.zoominfo. com). You can get contact information, summaries about the company, and other data, for free.

Before you start contacting anyone, though, it's time to move to the next chapter, where we'll discuss more about how you can choose the job that best suits you, your skills, and your goals. You'll need to know what you do best and how you can highlight all you have to offer in your résumé.

CHAPTER 3

Know Your Skills

When you look through job ads, you're sure to wonder how well you'll fit in with the position and with the company. Are you qualified for the job? Do you have the right skill set? Will you like the job and get some satisfaction from the tasks you'll perform?

The only way to know for sure is to get the job and give it a try. But before you start applying for positions, you can still get a good sense of what kinds of jobs are the best for you.

So now it's test-taking time. There is no pass or fail on these tests. There are no right or wrong answers, but you will get a strong impression of which positions you'll enjoy and the types of jobs in which you're most likely to find success.

If your answers to these and other assessments suggest that the customer service field isn't right for you, don't take the answer as gospel. If a job in this field is what you've always dreamed about, use what you learn about yourself from these assessments to think about this particular job and decide if you want to continue searching for it. These questions are only to get you thinking and provide you with some insight into your preferences and your qualities. Only you can decide what path to take next.

I encourage you to take all the free, more comprehensive assessments that are available at the Web sites mentioned later in this chapter. But first try these questions here for a taste of what to expect. You'll see from these sample questions that similar assessments are painless and private. No one, including future employers, will see the answers. Only you will know your responses.

Your Skills

You probably know many of your skills and talents. You know what you're good at and what you're not. What can be harder to determine is how you can use those abilities for a job.

You can find many online quizzes that will ask you questions about your skills, and then offer a list of occupations that you should consider. Here are a few examples of the types of questions you might be asked:

QUESTION:

When you sit in front of a computer, you:

a. Feel at ease. You love working with different programs and there aren't many systems you haven't seen or at least read about.
b. Panic. You've never used a computer for work before, and you're not even sure of the difference between a "login" and a "password."

ANSWERS:

If you answered "a," you may have high computer skills, and a job working with computers may suit you. Some of the jobs you might consider include computer technician, computer support specialist, or data entry.

If you answered "b," computers make you more than a bit nervous, and you'll probably be better off with a job that involves more interaction with people and less with machines.

QUESTION:

When you're asked to do work with numbers, you:

a. Ask if anyone has a calculator. You don't even feel comfortable balancing your checkbook.
b. Get started. You've always had a natural ability with numbers, and you're able to do a fair amount of calculations in your head.

ANSWERS:

If you answered "a," you should probably steer clear of jobs that involve calculating anything, from a store's inventory to a restaurant bill. Perhaps a job as a marketing research analyst, someone who analyzes statistics to determine consumer preferences, would be a bad idea for you.

If you answered "b," you should seek positions that include working with numbers or other data. Work as a billing clerk, an insurance company representative, or someone selling financial products could be worth considering.

QUESTION:
When you're faced with a long list of to-do items, and you know you don't have a lot of time to get them done, you:

a. Start with one thing. You know you're not going to get enough done, but you can only concentrate on one task at a time.
b. Do a little of everything at once. You're able to manage several tasks simultaneously without losing focus. Plus, with so many things happening at once, you're not going to be bored.

ANSWERS:
If you answered "a," you need an environment where things are a bit more calm. You prefer quiet to get your work done, and too many distractions will lead to delays and you probably won't do your best possible work.

If you answered "b," high-pressure environments, full of controlled chaos, are where you excel. You love the action and constant movement. You might consider work in the publishing industry, where there are never-ending deadlines, in the emergency room of a hospital, or in a busy restaurant.

There are many online resources that will ask you questions similar to those above, and they'll provide you with a list of jobs that may fit your skills. (You can also find links to all the quizzes found in this chapter on the Esperanza USA Web site at www.esperanza.us.)

America's Career Info Net is a Web site sponsored by the U.S. Department of Labor. On the site, you'll find a Skills Profiler quiz, which will help you figure out which skills you have and which jobs fit your skill set. Based on the skills you enter, the quiz will offer job possibilities and tell you how well you would match with each. You can find the quiz at www.careerinfonet.org/acinet/skills/default.aspx?nodeid=20.

Another skills assessment test can be found on the ISEEK Web site. ISEEK stands for Internet System for Education and Employment Knowledge, a Minnesota-based site. But you don't have to live in Minnesota to benefit from the site's skill test. Here you'll rate your skills and the test will offer career possibilities based on your answers. You can find the quiz at www.iseek.org/sv/12398.jsp.

The Web Site CareerKey has yet another quiz that will help you identify your skills and how they may relate to certain jobs. The site is offered by Lawrence K. Jones, a professor emeritus at North Carolina State University who specializes in career counseling and development. The quiz can be found at www.careerkey.org/asp/your_personality/take_test.asp.

Your Strengths and Weaknesses

You're likely to succeed at a job, or anything in life, if you know your strengths and weaknesses. Strengths might include an ability to stay organized, to multitask, and even to be on time. Or perhaps some of those qualities are among your weaknesses.

Learning more about your strengths and weaknesses will not only help you sell yourself to a potential employer, but also will remind you of areas where you can improve yourself to be more marketable to employers.

Here are some questions to help you uncover your strengths and your weaknesses:

QUESTION:
Your boss's secretary is home sick and you're answering his phone for the day. A very important client calls, furious, about a recent transaction. You listen to five minutes of ranting before you get a chance to say a word. Your boss is away from her desk. You:

a. Nicely tell the client that your boss has stepped away from her desk and you'll give her the message when she returns.

b. Do your best to calm the client. Show him you understand why he's upset, and while you weren't involved in the transaction and you have no power to make things right, you assure the client that he is very important to your boss, and your boss will do what it takes to correct the problem.

ANSWERS:

If you answered "a," you may not be much of a "people person." Confrontations make you nervous and you avoid them at all costs. You're best suited for a job that doesn't deal with outside clients or customers.

If you answered "b," you're a charmer and you were meant for customer service, client relations, or any job that allows you to use your personality to make amends. Communication is a big strength for you.

QUESTION:

Your boss tells you that because of problems with the company's most recent project, your department is over budget. You're assigned the task of finding places to cut back. You:

a. Take a look at the department's upcoming project, seeking places to save money next time. You then obtain a copy of the over-budget project's financial records to see where things went wrong, and you set up a meeting with the project leader to break down the mistakes. Finally, you write a memo about what the department can do better next time.

b. Stare at your boss, having no idea how to attack this problem.

ANSWERS:

If you answered "a," you're a problem-solver, something that should top the list of your strengths, and you should highlight that when you meet a prospective employer.

If you answered "b," you're not comfortable taking the initiative, and that's okay. You may be better off in a job that classifies you as a "soldier" rather than a "general."

QUESTION:
Your child receives a dollhouse for her birthday. It's got 78 pieces, 18 screws, 41 sticker decals, and 6 knobs that you can't identify. Your daughter can't wait to play with it, and she's bouncing with anticipation. You:

a. Start reading the directions, in between your child's questions and her poking at the pieces, and you begin putting together the dollhouse, knowing it will take the better part of the hour.

b. Begin putting it together with the goal of getting it done fast. Forget the directions, even if the parts aren't perfectly put together and not every decal is in place. Besides, your daughter won't have the patience to wait an hour, and she probably won't notice the difference.

ANSWERS:
If you answered "a," you pay great attention to detail. Work as an editor, an event planner, or a decorator would benefit from this quality.

If you answered "b," you're more interested in getting the job done quickly than you are getting it done perfectly. You should avoid job postings that require being detail-oriented and meticulous.

For more quizzes to help you determine your strengths and weaknesses, head to your computer:

Monster.com's Job Assets & Strengths Profiler is one of the most comprehensive online quizzes you can take. After asking a series of questions about what you're good at and what you're not, it offers a personalized report that includes your work personality, your leadership skills, and which traits, or "unique strengths," as the quiz calls them, you have. After your strengths are identified by the quiz, you can check out the Web site's job postings to see which jobs might fit your strengths. The quiz can be found at www.my.monster.com/JobStrengthProfile/Intro.aspx.

The Adult Pathways for Learning Quiz (on the Dr. Spock child wellness Web site) asks questions that will provide clues about your strengths and weaknesses. When the quiz is over, you'll see a chart that rates different parts of your intelligence (you might score high at musical abilities but poorly on interpersonal and emotional skills). While this quiz won't outwardly tell you what job you'd be best at, it will highlight certain personality traits that you may be able to apply to certain jobs. You can find the quiz at www.drspock.com/toolsforyou/son/0,2020,35,00.html.

Your Likes and Dislikes

Your interests may play a large role in how much you like a job. Sure, you may qualify for a position as an office manager, but if the thought of being stuck inside a place of work all day isn't attractive to you, you may end up hating your job, even if you're good at it. If you love the outdoors, you should find a job that allows you to feel the sunshine, such as working in a garden center or on a construction site.

Answer these quiz questions to learn more about what you like and dislike:

QUESTION:
Your neighbor is going on a job interview and he asks if you approve of his clothing choices. You:

a. Carefully look at what he is wearing and think he's making a big mistake. You invite yourself into his closet to find more suitable attire. You even coordinate his shoes and his socks for him.
b. Glance at him and say he looks fine, not seeing anything wrong with what he's wearing.

ANSWERS:
If you answered "a," you take an interest in fashion and you may be good at it, too. Work in clothing stores, as a personal shopper, or in sales will let you do what you love.

If you answered "b," you may not take much of an interest in clothing trends or what's hot this year. There's nothing wrong with that, but make sure you don't have to make those kinds of decisions on your next job.

QUESTION:

You take a job in an electronics store, and a customer starts asking about a television that's for sale. The television in the store is playing a hot movie that you've seen. The customer said he loved the film and he tries to strike up a conversation about the characters. You:

a. Have plenty to add to the conversation. It's fun to chat with strangers and you're always curious about what people have to say.

b. Listen politely for a moment and then tell the customer you need to do something in the storeroom.

ANSWERS:

If you answered "a," you're not shy about meeting new people and you're genuinely interested in what they have to say. *Outgoing* is another word for that type of personality. Public relations, marketing, or sales may be right for you.

If you answered "b," jobs that require you to make conversation with strangers should be crossed off your list. It doesn't matter whether it's because you're shy or because you're just not comfortable talking a lot around new people. You should stick with a job that keeps you away from customers and clients.

QUESTION:

Your home needs some work. The priority job is outside, fixing one of the loose bricks on your front steps. You're afraid someone could get hurt when the brick finally separates from the rest of the structure. You:

a. Look in the local paper for a handyman who will do the job inexpensively.

b. Head to the hardware store for mortar to stick in between the bricks and other tools to do the job yourself. You're no mason, and even though mixing and applying the mortar is a messy job, you enjoy the challenge and satisfaction you get from it.

ANSWERS:

If you answered "a," you might not like working with your hands. You'd be better suited in an office environment where the messiest thing you'd have to fix is the photocopy machine.

If you answered "b," you think it's nice to fix something, to make something, to get your hands dirty. Consider jobs in construction or home remodeling, carpentry, automotive repair, or working in a ceramics studio.

Here are some helpful online quizzes to help you assess your likes and dislikes:

The Princeton Review, a company that offers test preparation services, has a useful Career Quiz on its Web site. It will assess your personality through a series of questions about what types of jobs you think you'd prefer, and how you'd react in certain workplace situations. You can find the quiz at http://www.princetonreview.com/cte/quiz/career_quiz1.asp.

Monster.com has a quiz designed to help you find the perfect career according to your personality type. The quiz, called Discover Your Perfect Career, can be found at http://tools.monster.com/perfectcareer. It will ask about your personality and then give you career suggestions based on the qualities you choose in the quiz.

On a little different path, Monster.com has a What's Your Workstyle? quiz that's sure to give you some ideas about the type of workplace you'd like to be in every day. You can find the quiz at http://tools.monster.com/quizzes/workstyle.

You Have More Skills Than You Think

If you don't have a lot of professional work experience, you still have plenty of skills you can offer an employer. You just have to identify your skills in your everyday activities and learn how to present them professionally, for an employer to see. Here's an example.

Say you're active in your church, and you were involved in Christmas and Easter congregation gatherings. You feel like it's not impressive, but in making a checklist of everything you did, and putting the tasks in terms that apply to the workplace, you'll find you've used many talents for these activities, such as:

❏ For three consecutive years I was in charge of organizing the Christmas and Easter dinners for the parish church where I worship.

❏ These were the principal annual fund-raising events for our institution.

❏ Coordinated the events by attending meetings with the board and helping to develop the format for each function.

❏ Logged, distributed, and maintained progress control of all sales commitments and payments.

❏ Communicated regularly with volunteers to offer marketing tips to enhance their sales performance.

❏ Managed the affair itself, including contacting the venue where the events were held, selecting the menu, negotiating the costs, arranging entertainment, supervising the design, production, and printing of all collateral materials (informational flyer, invitation, tickets, and menus), orchestrating an appropriate color scheme, and ordering the decorations (centerpieces and additional flowers).

Wow. That's an action-packed list of skills and talents that are pretty impressive. Take another look at all the words that would catch the eye of a potential employer: *organize, fund-raising, coordinate, marketing, negotiate, arrange,* and so on, valuable experience that shows you can function in a professional capacity, getting multiple jobs done—all without official workplace experience.

So if you haven't spent a lot of time in the workplace, consider some of these items and see if you can create a skill list based on your experiences:

❏ Volunteering, from local hospitals to Girl Scouts to other charitable organizations

❏ Community activities/neighborhood watch groups
❏ Babysitting
❏ Church activities
❏ Parent/teacher associations
❏ School fund-raising, such as bake sales or other product sales
❏ Sports clubs and organizations associated with other hobbies
❏ Organizing a book club with friends
❏ Coupon and bargain-hunting talents

LANGUAGE

One important skill that you may be overlooking is language. English may be your second language, and you might consider that a drawback for you. Wrong. You're in the enviable position of being bilingual, a quality that more employers value.

According to a 2005 study (the Korn/Ferry International Executive Recruiter Index), 79 percent of executive recruiters—the people who do the hiring for many firms—say Spanish is the language most in demand by employers.

Throughout the United States, more and more people are speaking Spanish. And according to the Hispanic Association on Corporate Responsibility, Hispanics and Latinos have $380 billion of spending power. Companies are trying to accommodate this new customer base and they want to tap into those dollars. From customer service centers to government agencies, more organizations are hiring workers who speak English and Spanish. Health care, financial services, and sales and marketing are among the biggest areas of growth for Spanish speakers.

While your Spanish-speaking abilities are an asset, keep in mind that employers can demand fluency in English. Showing strength in both languages will give you an advantage in the workplace.

If you're specifically looking for jobs that need bilingual workers, check out the Bilingual Jobs Web site at www.bilingual-jobs.com/default_new.htm.

Getting Additional Training/Education

Looking at your skills and job preferences, you may discover that you need some additional training or education to pursue the work you want. If that's the case, here are some considerations:

COLLEGE

A college education can be the ticket to a higher-level, higher-paying position. But if you need to be working to support yourself and your family, it may be hard, if not logistically impossible, to attend college full-time.

You don't have to be a full-time student to get a college degree. Consider going part-time or in the evenings. Most schools offer special programs for students who need to work during the daytime. Get information about community and junior colleges in your area. They tend to cost less money, often have special programs in the evenings or on weekends, and focus on training for particular types of jobs.

If you're not interested in getting a degree, you may still want to take a few college classes, simply to get more specialized knowledge in a particular field.

You might even be able to get your employer to pay for college, especially if the skills you'd learn would help you advance at work, giving your boss a more valuable employee. This benefit, usually called a tuition reimbursement program, means you pay for your classes up front. As long as you get a passing grade, your employer will pay you back the cost of tuition and supplies.

TRADE SCHOOL/VOCATIONAL SCHOOL

Trade and vocational schools offer specialized instruction for a particular type of job. You'll find schools that offer classes to teach you how to style hair, fix cars, or learn plumbing, for example. These hands-on schools will give you the skills, also called applied skills, needed for many types of jobs.

These schools can also provide great contacts for you to find a job, because most claim successful job placement programs.

Research these schools carefully. While many are reputable, others aren't able to meet their promises for job placement and they can leave you with student loans and no way to pay for them. Find out what percentage of graduates are placed in jobs. Speak to former students and graduates of the school to find out about their experiences and if they'd recommend the school.

COMMUNITY EDUCATION

You can also find specialized classes in your community. Your local library, for example, may offer a training class in computers. Or, certain stores may offer free or low-cost classes—such as a consumer electronics store offering computer software training classes. They're of course hoping you'll buy products after taking the class, but usually there's no obligation to do so.

INTERNSHIPS

Businesses are often looking for cheap or free labor, so they hire students as interns. Internships are lower than entry-level jobs, and interns in some fields don't even get paid. Instead, they benefit from the experience of working firsthand in the field of their choice. Television news interns, for example, don't get paid, but they get to experience what it takes to put together a news program.

If there's an industry you want to learn more about and you can find the time to work part-time as an intern, you'll learn invaluable skills for the jobs of your choice. You'll also make great contacts who, if they like you and are impressed by your work, may hire you for regular-paying jobs in the future.

The Next Step

Any additional experience, education, or training you get will bolster your résumé. That's the next step—creating a résumé that spotlights your best qualities so you can get a job.

CHAPTER 4

Prepare Your Résumé

A résumé is far more than a listing of all the jobs you've ever held. It's an enormous tool to get you in the door for a job interview. It's a profile of who you are, professionally, and it's your chance to get a potential employer to notice you and want to learn more about you.

Your résumé is your opportunity to present all your best qualities and skills, but it's not a full autobiography. Résumés should be brief and to the point. Employers don't have hours to read through detailed résumés that are as long as a dissertation. In fact, within ten to fifteen seconds of looking at your résumé, most employers will decide if it belongs in the discard pile or if you're worth a closer look.

Choose Your Résumé Format

Before you start writing your résumé, you have to decide which kind of format you want to use. The one you choose may depend on the kind of experience you have and whether or not you've been in the workforce for a while.

CHRONOLOGICAL RÉSUMÉS

Chronological résumés are the most common. This kind of résumé lists all your work experience, with the most recent at the top of the "Work Experience" section (we'll talk more about the different sections of a résumé later in this chapter).

If you've been working for a while, and you have no hard-to-explain gaps in your work history, this is probably the résumé style for you. It will showcase how you've developed over the years, as you've moved from job to job.

The main advantage of a chronological résumé is that it's easy for employers to read, so they can quickly scan through your experience. Because it's so common, many employers expect to see this kind of résumé.

If you haven't had many jobs, are just out of college, or if you've been out of work for long periods of time, this probably is the wrong format for you. The gaps in your work history, or the shortness of it, e.g., if you are just out of college, will stand out with a chronological résumé.

You'll find an example of a chronological résumé on page 34.

FUNCTIONAL RÉSUMÉS

Functional résumés are organized by areas of expertise (such as "Management" or "Customer Service") instead of giving a job-by-job history. Under each category, you can explain the skills you have in that area.

This kind of résumé works best for certain situations:

- ❏ If you've jumped a lot from job to job, and you don't want an employer to get the impression you have a short attention span.
- ❏ If there were large time spans when you weren't working. (You don't have to give employment dates in this type of résumé.)
- ❏ If you want to change fields and you have little or no experience in the field in which you're applying for a job.
- ❏ If you have little professional work experience and you want your résumé to showcase your volunteer work and other unpaid experience.

If you're trying to show your experience—or lack of experience—in the best possible light, a functional résumé will allow you to draw attention to your best qualities while downplaying anything your résumé may be lacking. An example of a functional résumé appears on page 35.

Chronological Résumé

Yvette Gonzales
100–000 34th Street
New York, NY 10016
(212) 555-5555
Yvette_Gonzales@email.com

Objective   Seeking to use my seven years of experience and strong organizational and communication skills in a senior-level administrative assistant position.

Work History

Executive Administrative Assistant

July 2004 to present   Brown and Josephson, Inc.   New York, NY

Offer seamless office management for this law office while reporting directly to the company president. Accomplishments and duties include:
- Created the first database ever used by this office to organize past and present legal cases.
- Coordinate daily scheduling of clients, court dates, and other legal meetings.
- Field important phone calls from potential clients, directing them to the proper attorney with the firm, and ensuring their cases are managed with sensitivity and confidentiality.
- Direct pool of ten secretaries, working for eighteen attorneys. Proofread and edit all correspondence requested of the secretarial pool, including interoffice and client memos.

Secretary

May 2000 to July 2004   Brown and Josephson, Inc.   New York, NY

In a support environment, completed legal documents and summarized case files for staff attorneys. Filed and organized documents for ongoing cases and trials as needed by staff attorneys. Assisted paralegals with research for current cases. Promoted to Executive Administrative Assistant.

Key Skills

Computer	*Front Office*
- MS Word	- Reception
- MS Publisher	- Supervisor of secretarial pool
- MS Excel	- Typing: 85 words/minute
- MS PowerPoint	- Scheduling of appointments
- Adobe Photoshop/Illustrator	- Manage conference room schedule

Education

City University of New York, Associate's Degree in Office Management, 2006

Functional Résumé

Yvette Gonzales
100–000 34th Street
New York, NY 10016
(212) 555-5555
Yvette_Gonzales@email.com

Objective Seeking to use my seven years of experience and strong organizational and communication skills with new opportunities in the health care field.

Key Skills

Office Skills
- Able to coordinate daily scheduling of clients and court dates, ensuring there are no overlaps in conference room usage or attorney assignments.
- Direct pool of ten secretaries, working for eighteen attorneys.
- Versatile computer skills in all popular programs, including MS Office.
- File and organize confidential and highly sensitive legal documents for ongoing and completed cases.

Communication and Writing Skills
- Proofread and edit all correspondence requested of the secretarial pool, including interoffice and client memos.
- Field phone calls from potential clients, directing them to the proper attorneys.
- Research case law under paralegal supervision.

Interpersonal Skills
- Friendly, outgoing, caring.
- As an executive administrative assistant in a law firm, the sensitivity of client cases was paramount and an essential task.

Accomplishments
- Created the first database ever used by this office to organize past and present legal cases.

Work History

Executive Administrative Assistant
July 2004 to present   Brown and Josephson, Inc.   New York, NY

Secretary
May 2000 to July 2004   Brown and Josephson, Inc.   New York, NY

Education

City University of New York, Associate's Degree in Office Management, 2006

Combination Résumé

Yvette Gonzales
100–000 34th Street
New York, NY 10016
(212) 555-5555
Yvette_Gonzales@email.com

Objective Seeking to use my seven years of experience and strong organizational and communication skills with new opportunities in the health care field.

Key Skills

Computer
- MS Word
- MS Publisher
- MS Excel
- MS PowerPoint
- Adobe Photoshop/Illustrator

Front Office
- Reception
- Supervisor of secretarial pool
- Typing: 85 words/minute
- Scheduling of appointments
- Manage conference room schedule

Communication and Writing Skills
- Proofread and edit all correspondence requested of the secretarial pool, including interoffice and client memos.
- Field phone calls from potential clients, directing them to the proper attorneys.
- Research case law under paralegal supervision.

Interpersonal Skills
- Friendly, outgoing, caring.
- As an executive administrative assistant in a law firm, the sensitivity of client cases was paramount and an essential task.

Accomplishments
- Created the first database ever used by this office to organize past and present legal cases.

Work History

Executive Administrative Assistant

July 2004 to present   Brown and Josephson, Inc.   New York, NY

Offer seamless office management for this law office while reporting directly to the company president. Accomplishments and duties include scheduling and organizing client meetings, court dates and other legal meetings, and conference room usage. Also field phone calls from potential clients, and supervise secretarial pool. Previously served as secretary from May 2000 through July 2004. Duties included completing legal documents, summarizing case files for staff attorneys, filing and organizing documents for ongoing cases and trials, and assisting paralegals with research for current cases.

Education

City University of New York, Associate's Degree in Office Management, 2006

COMBINATION RÉSUMÉS

A combination résumé is part functional, part chronological. This résumé is helpful if there are certain skills you want an employer to notice right away and most clearly. It has the same sections you'd write for the other types of résumés, starting with categories for your areas of expertise, followed by your work history.

Combination résumés may work if:

- You're a graduating student. You can highlight your skills, especially if you don't have much work history.
- You haven't been working for some time. Again, by highlighting your skills, you downplay your lack of employment in recent years.

You may want to create more than one résumé, for use with different kinds of job applications. The basic information in all three types is similar, so once you write the first version, at most you'll be reordering the information and not completely rewriting.

Tips Before You Begin

Here are some other items to keep in mind before you actually start writing your résumé.

- **Keep notes:** The quizzes in chapter 3 should have helped you narrow down some of the items you'll want to add to your résumé. You'll of course need your work history, but additionally, you want to share skills and qualities you have, other than those listed in your job descriptions. Create and keep handy a list of your skills and your strengths. As you write your résumé, refer back to the list and make sure you're including everything that may impress a potential employer.
- **Be crisp:** Your résumé shouldn't be cute or too unusual, but you do want it to be crisp. The first time most résumés are looked at by employers, they're only skimmed, and judged on what jumps out, or doesn't. Your résumé needs to offer clear sections so an employer

can quickly find the information he needs to make a fast decision about you. You want it to stand out because of how it's organized, not because you chose to use purple paper, uncommon fonts, or other unusual tactics.

❏ **Don't be repetitive:** Perhaps you've held three jobs with different companies, but your duties were very similar. As you write, you may find you're using the same words over and over again. Try using a variety of words to describe similar tasks. For example, instead of saying "managed," consider using "oversaw" or "led." If you're having trouble, use a thesaurus or check Appendix A of this book, which gives a list of words commonly used in résumés.

❏ **Keep the personal, well, personal:** Information about marital status, how many kids you have, your hobbies, and other personal items don't belong on a résumé. Some of these things could come up in an interview, and you need to know what's legal for a recruiter to ask and what's not. We'll talk more about that in chapter 6.

❏ **Proofread:** This is one of the most important things you can do for your résumé. You don't want to give an employer a résumé that has misspellings or grammar mistakes. If your résumé is sloppy, it will reflect poorly on you. If you feel your grasp of English isn't perfect, consider asking a friend to proofread your résumé. You can also find someone to check your résumé for errors at one of the Labor Department's Career One-Stop centers (www.careeronestop.org or call 1-877-US-2JOBS).

❏ **Stick to one page:** Few résumés need to be longer than one page. If you have a very long work history, it's probably safe to eliminate your oldest jobs. Or you can use a different format—one that takes less space—for the oldest positions.

Writing Your Résumé

No matter what résumé format you've chosen, many of its pieces will be the same.

CONTACT INFORMATION

Start with your contact information. This includes your name, address, telephone number, and e-mail address. If you're a college student and you have a school address and a permanent address, give both.

It's not recommended that you supply your current work telephone number or work e-mail address. (If you're not respectful to your employer today, future bosses may have doubts about how respectful you'd be to him or her someday.) Instead, provide either your home phone or cell phone and e-mail. Several times during the day, if you're at work, use your break time to check your messages.

Your contact information should be at the top of your résumé page, either centered or justified to the left side of the page.

OBJECTIVE

A heading titled "Objective" may be the next item on your résumé, though most professional résumé writers say it's optional. An "Objective" section explains the kind of work you're looking for. It should be clear and concise, expressing your career goal, or at least the goal you're trying to reach with this résumé. It should be no longer than three or four lines.

Some examples of how an "Objective" might read:

OBJECTIVE: To use my customer relations and organizational skills in a hotel management position.

OBJECTIVE: Seeking a Registered Nurse position in the emergency room, where I can use both domestic nursing experience and my talents obtained as a field nurse for the Army Reserves.

OBJECTIVE: To use my background in employee benefits and my sharp communication skills in a human resources position.

OBJECTIVE: Seeking an office manager position where I can use the skills I've developed as an executive secretary.

When you're writing your objective, make sure it's forward-thinking and not simply a rehash of your past experience.

CAREER SUMMARIES AND QUALIFICATIONS SUMMARIES

Instead of using an objective, many job seekers instead use a "Career Summary" or a "Qualifications Summary." This section replaces an objective by offering an overview of your experience. This could be one sentence or several, using strong action words to boast what you have to offer.

Some examples of a "Career Summary" or a "Qualifications Summary":

QUALIFICATIONS SUMMARY: Named "Teacher of the Year" three years in a row. Ninety-eight percent of my students in the past five years have passed their state exams.

CAREER SUMMARY: A results-oriented customer service manager with strong planning and critical thinking skills. Demonstrated dramatic increase in customer satisfaction.

A potential employer should read your summary and be impressed enough to call you to learn more.

WORK HISTORY

If you're writing a chronological résumé, this is where you list your work history. By work history we mean all work history, including part-time jobs, volunteering, and any work you've done, whether or not it relates to the position you're seeking.

This section can go by several names: "Work Experience," "Experience," "Work History," "Employment," or even "Professional History."

Each job entry should include your title, your dates of employment, and a description of your duties. As you write, remember to use strong action words (see Appendix A for suggestions). If you plan to post your résumé online, know that potential employers search résumé databases using keywords—words that describe qualities the employer wants in an employee. So use the words you think an employer wants to see for a particular industry.

Start with your present job, if you have one, and go backward in time. Entries might look like this:

Work History

Sales Representative

1/04 to present   ABC Clothing Store   Philadelphia, PA

Responsible for increasing product sales by creating coordinated outfit designs for customers. Create display areas near registers and design window displays. Named Salesperson of the Month for April, June, and September 2004.

Retail Clerk

5/03 to 1/04   XYZ Clothing Store   Philadelphia, PA

Duties included processing customer transactions upon checkout. Offered additional products to customers from display areas. Offered and processed credit card offers to customers.

If you're using a functional résumé, your "Skills" section might look something likes this:

Skills

Sales: Increase product sales by offering accessory items to customers. Use strategies such as carrying their potential purchases to a fitting room ahead of time, encouraging customers to try clothing on. Frequently named Salesperson of the Month.

Customer service: Using eye contact and a friendly manner, greet customers and offer assistance. Direct customers to proper sizes and help find items to coordinate clothing purchases.

Displays: Create both window displays and product outlays near registers to increase sales. Design themes for holidays, back-to-school, and other events.

You can find more examples of job descriptions in the résumés presented earlier in this chapter.

WORK HISTORY CONCERNS

If you feel something in your work history may cause concerns for employers, here are some suggestions to improve your résumé:

❑ **If you're a student:** If you've been going to school so you haven't had much work experience, or if you haven't had experience in the field you'd like to pursue, use your educational experiences to bolster your résumé. Add a special heading with "Relevant Classes" or "College Projects" to list activities that pertain specifically to the job you're trying to get.

❏ **If you have employment gaps:** If you're returning to work after years of being at home, think of activities you were involved in when you weren't working. This is a great place to add volunteer and charity work, or special education or training. If you only had a few months where you were unemployed, consider eliminating the use of months when you give dates for your employment history. If you were out of the workforce for years because you were a stay-at-home parent or caring for an elderly family member, be honest. While you weren't at work, you were performing some very important duties. Employers have families, too. They'll understand your absence.

❏ **If you've had too many jobs:** If you've jumped from job to job because you've gotten bored easily, that could be a bad thing. But if you've had a lot of movement because of promotions or training opportunities, that could show you're aggressive and hardworking. If your work history list is too long for your tastes, consider using a functional résumé instead of a chronological one.

KEY SKILLS

In the "Key Skills" section, you have a chance to stress your best qualities and talents. These should be skills that employers value, ranging from language aptitudes and communication skills, to problem-solving expertise and beyond. This section is a great opportunity for you to offer detail about what you're best at.

The "Key Skills" section may be the place you make the biggest changes if you're tailoring your résumé for each job to which you apply. When you read a job posting, make sure you add qualities that the employer is looking for to your "Key Skills" section, if you have those skills.

Here's an example of how a "Key Skills" section might read:

Key Skills

- Proficient in English, Spanish, and Portuguese
- Practiced in sales presentations
- Expertise in direct marketing campaigns

Or, you could use a more specific heading, if that's what suits your experience. For example, instead of "Key Skills," use "Computer Skills."

Computer Skills

- MS Word
- MS Publisher
- MS Excel
- MS PowerPoint
- Adobe Photoshop/Illustrator

EDUCATION/TRAINING

Here is where you'll list your education and other training. You should name the school, when you graduated or completed a program, and what kind of degree you earned. If you have more than one degree, put the most recent one first. For example:

Education:

5/2003   State University of New York   Binghamton, NY
Bachelor of Arts, Art History
3.5 GPA

6/1999   Valley Stream Central High School   Valley Stream, NY
Regent's Diploma

If you didn't go to college but instead attended a technical school, vocational school, or other training, you should put that here, too.

Education:

10/2003   The New School   New York, NY
Criminal Justice and the Law: Completed this three-day workshop.

5/2000   Katherine Gibbs School   Norristown, PA
Criminal Justice Associate in Applied Science

6/1998   Manalapan/Englishtown High School   Manalapan, NJ
High School Diploma

If a high school equivalency diploma is your highest education, be proud and put it on your résumé. It shows that you have what it takes to do what you have to do to get the job done.

OTHER RÉSUMÉ ADDITIONS TO CONSIDER

Depending on your experience and your special talents, you may want to add some extra headings to your résumé. Here are some to think about:

Awards: If you've won any awards or commendations
Published work: If your work has ever appeared in a magazine or other publication
Public speaking: If you've given workshops or other speeches
Accomplishments: If you've worked on successful projects you want to highlight
Affiliations: Memberships in professional organizations or unions
Languages: If you didn't add this to the "Key Skills" section, you can create a separate "Languages" heading
Other benefits: If you're willing to work overnight hours or travel or are planning to pursue more education—anything that might make you a more desirable employee

A Word About Credit Reports

If you have bad credit, it can affect more than your ability to get a loan. It could stop you from getting a job.

Employers often look at a potential employee's credit report before deciding if they're going to offer a job. It is a way of measuring your fiscal responsibility over a period of years.

The Federal Trade Commission says that according to the Fair Credit Reporting Act (FCRA), an employer must get your permission to look at your credit report. It's probably in your best interest to say yes, even if you're a little worried about what the employer might see. If you say no, and you have every right to, the employer is likely to suspect some strange activity and may be leery about hiring you.

If you don't get a job because of information in your report, the employer must show you the report and tell you how to get a copy from the consumer reporting company. There is no charge for the report if you request it within sixty days of getting notice that you did not get the job.

Everyone is entitled by law to see a copy of their credit report once a year. To get yours, visit the Web site www.annualcreditreport.com or click the link on the Esperanza USA Web site (www.esperanza.us), or call toll-free 877-322-8228. It's essential that you know what's in your report and take steps to correct any problems. You certainly don't want to lose out on a job opportunity because of bad credit.

For more on how to improve your credit, check out our book *How to Fix Your Credit*, available on the Esperanza Web site.

CHAPTER 5

The Cover Letter, Recommendation Letters, and Phone Calls

Cover Letters

When you send your résumé to a prospective employer, you have to introduce yourself. You make your introduction using what's called a cover letter. Before an employer sees your résumé, he or she will see your cover letter.

A cover letter is another way for you to distinguish yourself from all the other people applying for the job you want. When an employer is looking to fill a position and is deluged with dozens of résumés, usually a few stick out as worthy of an interview. In this pile of résumés, some people may have more qualifications than you, but if you impress a recruiter with your cover letter, he or she just might want to meet you.

Whether you're applying for a job via e-mail or on paper, you need to use your cover letter as an opportunity to capture an employer's attention.

WHAT A COVER LETTER CAN DO FOR YOU

Imagine an employer sitting at her desk, deep in thought and hopeful about who she will hire for the position she needs to fill. In front of her lies a stack of résumés. Lots of neat white paper, potential employees, with experience of all kinds. They all want the job.

She begins sorting, one pile for people she'd like to interview, one pile for those who don't qualify. Some of the cover letters simply say, "Dear Sir/Madam, I think I'd be a great candidate for this job. My résumé is attached." Not very exciting, thinks the employer.

Then she comes to a cover letter that's different. It tells her why she wants to hire this applicant. This applicant stands out. The letter shows confidence. It shows her that this person belongs on the "interview" side of the desk.

A cover letter should be more than a rehash of your résumé. Employers won't be impressed by your letter if you simply rewrite job descriptions.

Instead, view the cover letter as an opportunity. You can highlight qualities about yourself that you had trouble fitting into your résumé. You can show that you know how to write complete sentences and communicate. You can show that you want the job and that you'd be a great contender.

COVER LETTER DOS

Some things are expected by employers in a cover letter. Here are the items you should think about when preparing to write yours. (After you've written your cover letter, come back to this list and make sure you haven't forgotten anything.)

Paper

- Your cover letter and résumé should both be written on high-quality, $8\frac{1}{2} \times 11$ paper.
- Use a color paper that's easy on the eyes, such as white or cream. Don't get overly creative.
- Type your letter and make it look professional. If you don't have a computer, ask a friend for help or use a computer at a local library. Typewriters work, too, no matter how old-fashioned they might seem today.

Contact Information

- The first item on a cover letter is contact information—yours and the employer's. (Look at the sample cover letter on page 50 to see the proper format for a business letter.)
- Make sure you spell the employer's name correctly and that you're using *Mr.* for men and *Ms.* for women. If the person's first name could be male or female, call the company and ask the operator or receptionist.
- If an ad doesn't give the name of the employer, try to get it. Call the company and ask. If you still can't find it, consider "Dear Sir or Madam," "To Whom It May Concern," or even "Dear Hiring Manager."

Language

- Be a bit formal, so avoid contractions, such as "it's," "don't" or "I've."
- It's easy to start each sentence with "I" when you're talking about yourself. Try to use some variety and make sure to use active sentences. For example, instead of "This job showed me how to . . ." say "On this job, I learned . . ."
- As with your résumé, if you're not sure that your English is proper, ask someone to proofread your letter, such as a friend or a job counselor at a Career One-Stop Center. A grammar or spelling mistake in a cover letter could lose the job for you. Make this an opportunity to show you're a good writer.

The Body

- Before writing the letter, do some research on the company so you can personalize your letter to them.
- This is your chance to shine. Tell the employer which of your qualities and skills will make you a perfect fit for this job.
- If you're applying for a position for which you may not have enough experience, stress your positive traits and use the letter to explain that you're a go-getter, you're hardworking, and you're a fast learner.
- Refer back to the job ad and mention that some of the skills listed in the ad are skills that you possess.

Length

- One page, no longer.

The End:

- Before you sign off, ask for an interview. You can suggest times and dates that you're available. Don't be overbearing or pushy, but make it clear you're eager and can be accommodating.
- When you close your letter, use "Sincerely," "Yours Truly," or "Cordially."
- Make sure to sign it!

COVER LETTER DON'TS

- Don't repeat your résumé.
- Don't make grammar and spelling mistakes.
- Don't send the wrong letter to the wrong company. If you're not careful in customizing your letters, you may accidentally forget to change the employer's name or company name. You don't want to advertise to an employer that you're trying all over to get a job, even if that's the truth.
- Don't say anything negative about yourself. If you fear you don't have enough experience for the job, don't say that in the letter. Let the employer decide.
- Don't get personal. You don't need to reveal personal data, such as your marital status or how many children you have. In most cases, those facts are not relevant to a job search.
- Don't let a coffee stain travel to the employer's office. Be neat.
- Don't be ordinary. "Please consider me for the chef opening," and "I'm applying for the chef's job," are not exactly attention grabbers, and they could be the opening line in a cover letter for any applicant. Instead, try something like, "Your need for a chef and my two years of experience at Restaurant ABC make an excellent match."
- Don't forget to add any qualifications you have that match those mentioned in the ad.

WHAT COVER LETTERS SHOULD LOOK LIKE

Here's a template you may want to use to get started. You can also find other sample letters online at the job Web sites mentioned throughout the book, and Monster.com offers sample letters for specific occupations.

Your Address

City, State, Zip

Date

Mr./Ms. Name

Human Resources

Company Name

Company Address

City, State, Zip

Dear Mr./Ms. [Last Name],

Use this paragraph to make the employer interested in you, and show something to make you stand out from the dozens of others applying for the job. Explain that your experience matches the company's need for an employee, and that you're interested in the company.

Show yourself off here. Generally, list some of your skills and experience that fit the job posting. This paragraph should show the reader you have a lot to offer as an employee.

Talk in more detail about some of your on-the-job successes. Don't write too much here. You don't want to rewrite your résumé, but give highlights of your best accomplishments.

Tell the reader, as you finish your letter, that you're looking forward to hearing from them, or you will call soon for an appointment.

Sincerely,

[Your Signature]

Your Typed Name

Here's an example of a solid cover letter.

200–200 86th St.
New York, NY 10003

March 15, 2007

Mr. Jose Vega
Human Resources Manager
New York University Medical Center
550 First Avenue
New York, NY 10016

Dear Mr. Vega,

Your need for an Emergency Room staff nurse and my five years of experience in the ER at Long Island Jewish Medical Center (LIJ) seem to be a perfect match.

I'm a dedicated Registered Nurse with experience far beyond the ER. I've spent significant time in LIJ's Intensive Care Unit, Cardiac Care Unit, and Pediatrics Unit. After broadening my knowledge and performing well in various departments, I've learned my home is the ER. The fast pace is made for me, and I'm at my best juggling a variety of cases in the most trying of circumstances.

I've recently won awards for patient care and family satisfaction at LIJ, and the same qualities I've demonstrated there will travel with me wherever I go. I'd love to bring my strong initiative, my ability to work well with all levels of ER staff, and my energy to your hospital.

I believe I'd make a great contribution to New York University Medical Center. I've enclosed my résumé for your review. I look forward to the opportunity to discuss my skills further.

Sincerely,

Maria Vargas, R.N.

References

When someone is thinking about hiring you, they want to know if you're going to be a good worker. The best way they can learn more about you is to contact people you've worked for in the past. These former employers and colleagues are called your references.

References should be typed on a separate piece of paper from your résumé. It's as simple as writing the person's name, how they know you, and how long you've known each other.

Some job ads request that you send a reference list with your résumé. Others don't. It's smart to send references, even if the employer doesn't ask, because it shows you're serious and you have people on your team ready to speak on your behalf.

When you choose references, don't simply give a potential employer a list of names and phone numbers of people you've worked for in the past. You want to make sure you select references who like you and respect your work. You want them to have good things to say about you.

You should choose people who have been your immediate supervisors and who know about your skills, your attitude, and your work ethic. If you're tempted to use the company president as a reference because he has an important title, but you never directly worked with him, you're making a mistake. When a prospective employer calls, he won't have very much to say about you.

You can also use someone you haven't worked for directly but who knows your work anyway. For example, if you work in sales, a customer might have terrific experiences to share about you.

If you don't have a lot of work experience, don't put down the names of family members. Of course they'll have nice things to say about you. Consider using professors, community leaders, advisors, and other people who know you.

Before you give someone's name as a reference, make sure it's okay with them to be added to your list. Simply ask. Give them a copy of your résumé so they can have your career history and skills fresh in their minds.

Your reference list doesn't have to be fancy: names, titles, contact information, and how long you've know the person and in what capacity. Here's an example:

Reference List for Victor Garcia

Reference	Relationship	Years Known
Kevin Berns Supervisor, Limos-R-Us One Drivers Circle New York, NY 10006 ken@limos.com	Mr. Berns has been my supervisor since my start at the company. He can confirm my safe driving record, my high customer satisfaction ratings, and my ability to get to pickups on time.	3
Sharon Milano 4 10th St. New York, NY 10006 Sharon@aol.com	Ms. Milano has been a regular passenger of mine for two years. She can attest to my helpful nature, as I bring her to weekly medical appointments.	2
George Figueroa Super Drivers 110 Sixth Ave. New York, NY 10006 gfigueroa@superdrivers.com	Mr. Figueroa was my employer at TLC Cabs for three years. He can confirm my "Driver of the Month" awards and my willingness to work hard.	5

Letters of Recommendation

Letters of recommendation provide similar information to an employer as references, but you might prefer this approach instead. You'd be handing prospective employers letters directly from the people who know your work and who have nice things to say about you.

The advantage of using letters of recommendation is that a prospective employer may have bad luck using a reference list. What if your references are in meetings and they forget to return the phone call, or they're on maternity leave or away at a conference? You don't want a recruiter to be unable to reach your references.

Ask those people you would use as references if they'd write you a letter of recommendation, and consider sending those with copies of your résumé when you apply for a job.

Following Up with Phone Calls

After you send out your cover letter, résumé, and references, it's time to sit back and wait. But only for a little while.

If the employer calls you for an interview, terrific. You're on your way. But you can also take charge and call the employer.

If the job posting says "no phone calls," you should respect that. But if nothing is said about phone calls, you should follow up on your mailings. It can give you a competitive edge when you remind the employer of your interest in the job and will provide you another opportunity to make a good impression.

A week to ten days after you send your résumé is a good time to call. If you get the right person on the phone, remind them of who you are and what job you're interested in, and ask where they are in the hiring process. Note that the employer may be nowhere near making a decision, or a decision may have already been made to hire someone else. Be prepared for rejection, but also be prepared to answer questions about yourself in an on-the-spot telephone interview. (We'll talk more about interviews in the next chapter.)

If the employer says, "Thanks, but you're not right for the job," thank them for their candor and honesty, but then ask if there are other positions at the company you might be right for. You could also ask the interviewer why he or she thought you were a weak candidate for the job so you can learn how you might do better next time.

Don't be discouraged. Not everyone is right for every position. Even if you're turned down, remember you're making contacts and getting practice talking about yourself and what you can offer. And even though rejection can be hard, it's better to know if you're in the running or not so you can concentrate your energies where it will count.

Remember that "no" means "no," and you shouldn't get pushy. You shouldn't leave five messages a day for the hiring person. Persistence is a positive quality, but you don't want to turn them off by being overly aggressive. If they don't return your calls, take the hint and move on to the next opportunity.

Keep a Log

When you're on the hunt for a job, you're bound to get confused about all the résumés and cover letters you're sending out. You may see some job listings more than once on different Web sites and there are so many, they can be hard to remember. To ease the confusion, and so that you can be ready when the phone rings, keep a log of which ads you've answered and when.

Get a simple notebook and write a few columns. Something like this:

Employer	Job Description	Date Sent	Notes
ABC Company Jose Green 123 A Street Town, City, Zip Code	Hairdresser	Aug. 5	called on Aug. 12. Jose Green on vacation until Aug.17, call again.
XYZ Hair and Nails Maria Rodriguez 14 B Street Town, City, Zip Code	Haircutter	Aug. 5	called on Aug. 12. Maria Rodriguez said they're not setting up interviews yet. Call Aug. 20.
KLM Hairstyles Sarah McFarley 32-14 C Street Town, City, Zip Code	Hair Stylist	Aug. 5	called on Aug. 13. Job filled.

CHAPTER 6

Prepare for the Interview

Now is the moment you've been waiting for: the job interview. This is your opportunity to make yourself stand out as the candidate they want to hire. Show them what you're made of.

The Basics

Forget for a moment about what you're going to say and do when you arrive at your appointment. There are some items you need to consider first. Some may seem obvious, but they're as important as your résumé. You want to make a lasting impression in a positive way.

BE ON TIME
You don't want to start out your interview with an apology for lateness. Employers want employees to be on time, and they don't want excuses. If you're late for your interview, the employer might think you're tardy on a regular basis, and therefore he may assume you'll often be late for work.

If your interview is scheduled for 10 a.m., plan to be there at 9:50 a.m. Always try to be a little early. The employer may have some forms for you to fill out before the actual interview begins. If you're very early, you could always check out the neighborhood and get a cup of coffee.

Being on time means you're more likely to be relaxed when you arrive.

DON'T GET LOST

Get directions to the company when you set up your interview time, and if you forget, call back and ask the receptionist for the location. Or, you can look up the company location online and use services such as MapQuest.com for directions.

Whether you're driving or taking a bus or train, it's important to know exactly where you need to go and how long it will take to get there. If you're not familiar with the area where the company is located, take a trial run. Take notes on how to get where you're going and make sure to bring them on your interview day. You don't want to call the recruiter and say that you're lost when you're supposed to be meeting with him or her.

MAKE CONTINGENCY PLANS

If you have small children who need a babysitter when you go on your interview, or if you usually care for an elderly relative, you need to do some extra planning. Arrange for your kids' care with Babysitter A, and then call Babysitter B to make sure they'll be available if the first sitter has to cancel. If your kids are usually in school, make sure someone will be available to pick them up if they get sick. And finally, make sure someone can meet them after school in case your interview lasts longer than expected.

DRESS THE PART

You may consider the way you dress and the jewelry you wear to be part of how you express yourself. When you're on your own time, it is. But when you're at work, your employer may expect you to conform to the company's culture, also called corporate culture.

Companies spend a lot of money to establish their culture and their brand, and they expect their employees to fit in. Wearing a uniform, dressing more conservatively, or removing a nose earring while you're at work doesn't mean you're giving up a part of yourself or your culture. It's not a betrayal of your values to conform to your employer's expectations. In exchange for a salary, you're agreeing to abide by an employer's rules while you're working. When it's your own time, do as you wish.

For example, McDonald's wants its employees in uniforms, and they want customers to concentrate on the food they're buying, not on the nose ring worn by the cashier. Many workplaces expect conservative dress and would frown upon modern or youthful fashion, whether hip-hop, goth, hippie, or beachwear. Baggy pants, halter tops, and slippers may be fine in your community or in certain social venues, but not in most workplaces.

As a teenager, I went for a job interview at a well-known, trendy clothing store. I wore a dark-colored shirt and pants. It was an outfit that was common in New York, where I lived at the time. At my interview, the employer asked if I'd be willing to shop at the store and dress according to their style, which was generally considered more preppy, but would make me look like a stranger in my neighborhood. I needed the job, so for the second interview, I wore khaki pants, a light-colored button-down shirt, and a blue tie. I got the job, and I learned a great lesson. Looking preppy didn't change who I was, while adjusting to their demands allowed me to have a stable job that helped me pay for college. It was a trade-off that made me stronger.

So for your interview, dress the part. Look at the company and get an idea of its corporate culture: business attire and conservative dress are rarely frowned upon by an employer. Try to look like you fit in. You won't be changing your nature, but you'll be giving yourself an opportunity to join the group.

Remember, your work colleagues will learn about you and your culture through your personality. You won't be betraying yourself, or your culture, by your dress. This may be a difficult transition. Often it can bring about stress, not only from yourself as you try to "fit in" clothing-wise, but with friends and family. Many times spouses become concerned that your corporate image is "changing" you. Explain to anyone who asks that your changes are for your employer, but your soul and your spirit are still the same.

THE NOSE KNOWS

When you meet the interviewer for the first time, you want him or her to concentrate on what you have to say, not how you smell. Do your best to remove any distractions.

❏ **Cologne or perfume:** You may love a certain scent, but it could divert attention from what you're saying in an interview situation. The scent might even remind the interviewer of a former boyfriend or girlfriend, with whom they had a bad breakup. You don't need that reminder clouding the interviewer's vision of you.

❏ **Smoking:** If you're a smoker, try not to smoke for at least thirty minutes before your interview. The smell will stick to your clothing and skin and be noticed by the interviewer.

❏ **Breath mints:** Even if you brush your teeth regularly, you might suffer from bad breath. Have a mint before you go into your meeting (but make sure you're not chewing gum).

❏ **Body odor:** Many people who suffer from body odor don't even realize they have a problem. Use deodorant and do your best to be clean.

❏ **Hair and nails:** Make sure your hair is brushed and your nails are neat and clean.

Mentally Prepare

Going on a job interview makes most people nervous, no matter how successful they've been. Having butterflies in your stomach is understandable. You're thinking about how much you want this job and you don't want to mess up the opportunity.

Being nervous is okay, but there are steps you can take to help yourself relax. Feeling prepared will take you a long way.

RESEARCH

If you haven't done it already, research the company you're interviewing with. The more you know about the business, the more comfortable you'll feel. You'll be armed with the knowledge that you understand the company, its goals, and what it is likely to want from an employee.

Start online with a search engine such as Google.com or Yahoo! .com. Simply type the name of the company and see what you come up with. You may find some very useful news items about the company, or other information about marketing campaigns and product advertising. You can also read about the company and its mission on its own Web site. You can find either using a search engine or guess by using the company's name and a ".com" at the end.

What do you want to learn? Everything you can that may pertain to the job you're applying for.

PRACTICE INTERVIEW QUESTIONS

Think about the job you're applying for and try to anticipate what the employer may ask you. They're likely to ask you about your past jobs or other experience. Have a friend look at your résumé and ask you questions, as if you're on an interview.

There are many Web sites that offer common interview questions and suggested answers. You don't want to memorize what they say, but they're worth looking at for some ideas.

- ❏ College Grad: www.collegegrad.com
- ❏ Job Interview: www.job-interview.net
- ❏ Monster.com: www.monster.com

LEGAL AND ILLEGAL INTERVIEW QUESTIONS

Before you enter the interview, it's important for you to know that not every question an interviewer asks is legal. There are laws that have deemed some questions illegal for an interviewer to ask, especially personal questions that have nothing to do with the job in question. The government considers it to be discriminatory to ask about:

Race	Religion	Age
Color	National origin	Disability
Sex	Birthplace	Marital/family status

Just because an interviewer isn't supposed to ask illegal questions doesn't mean an interviewer won't. If an illegal question does arise, remember that you can control how much information you offer and what kind of information you discuss.

If an illegal topic comes up, try changing the subject or bringing the conversation back to something that's appropriate. If they ask, "How many kids do you have?" consider saying, "Kids are great, but my focus is this job opportunity." If they ask your age, skirt the question by talking about your experience, or say, "I'm old enough to know I'm excited about this job opportunity." If they ask what country you're from, tell them how much you love living in America and that you're looking forward to contributing to your community through this job.

The line between illegal and inappropriate is a tricky one. Here are some examples of questionable inquiries and how you may choose to deal with them:

- ❏ *"Where are you from?"* Employers are not allowed, thanks to the Civil Rights Act of 1964, to discriminate based on national origin. Similarly, it's illegal to ask, *"That's an unusual accent. Where do you come from?" "What's your native language?" "You have an unusual last name. Tell me about it."* If an interviewer asks in some way where you're from, illegally, you can respond by asking how your national origin has bearing on this job. For most jobs, it won't, and that's what makes the question illegal.

- ❏ *"What religion are you?"* For most jobs, your religion is irrelevant, and therefore asking the question is discriminatory. An exception may be if you're applying for a job at a religious institution. The institution may require that its employees be of that religion. Instead of answering, ask the interviewer why he or she wants to know.

- ❏ *"Are you married?"* Instead of asking outright, the interviewer may say, *"Do you prefer to be called Mrs., Ms., or Miss?"* The question in and of itself is not illegal, because no law protects you from discrimination based on marital status, but it certainly is inappropriate in most circumstances. In response, you could ask why the interviewer is asking the question. They may be making small talk, or there could be a bigger reason. They may be trying to decide if you're going to be distracted from work by personal issues. You could simply avoid answering directly, instead saying that your first commitment is to your career.

❏ *"Do you have children?"* or similarly, *"Are you planning to have kids?"* or *"Who takes care of your kids when you're working?"* also are not necessarily illegal questions, but the legality depends more on the reason behind the question. The interviewer may be trying to figure out if you're going to call in sick a lot because your child is home sick from school, or if you have a reliable babysitter for your working hours, or if you plan to take maternity leave soon. Though the question is inappropriate, you could tell the interviewer about your reliable child care, or answer that your job is your first priority, and never really say whether or not you have children.

❏ *"Please give us the name of someone to contact in case of an emergency."* Before you're hired, this question is inappropriate and could be a way for an interviewer to search for information about your marital status or even where your spouse works. You can answer by saying you don't have the phone numbers with you at this time, and that will probably be the end of that line of questioning.

You can always refuse to answer the question, but know you may not get the job if the interviewer isn't satisfied with your answer, or lack of answers. (Do you really want to work for someone who asks illegal questions, anyway?)

If you feel you've been denied a job because of discrimination, or because you answered illegal questions and you think they didn't like your answer, you have some recourse. The U.S. Equal Employment Opportunity Commission (EEOC) is a government agency charged with investigating claims of discrimination. To contact the EEOC, go online to www.eeoc.gov, or call 1-800-669-4000.

If you're concerned about a question that's been asked of you, think before running to the EEOC. Many interviewers may not realize a question is illegal, or they may not have had an ulterior motive in asking. Think about their intent before taking action.

BE CALM

If you're sitting in the waiting area before you're called for your interview and your heart keeps beating faster, try some techniques to calm yourself.

Start with breathing. It may sound like a silly idea, but slowing your breathing will help you relax. Breathe in through your nose and out slowly through your mouth. Count breaths while you do it. Concentrate, and you'll be able to distract yourself from your nerves.

Consider using prayer or asking for guidance from God, first to calm your nerves, and second to help you focus on the interview you're about to have. If you're nervous about having a meeting with an individual, take the time to share your anxiety with God. Think about it. You've just had a conversation with the Creator of everything there is. So going in to have a conversation with a regular person should be easy in comparison.

Have a positive outlook. You may be jittery and you may need this job, but the employer also needs to hire someone. And this isn't the only job opportunity you'll ever have. Even if you don't get the job, it's a learning experience and you'll be able to use your familiarity with the process to perform better next time. You've practiced and prepared for this moment. Don't forget to enjoy it.

What to Bring

When you go to your interview, bring a few items with you.

Take a few copies of your résumé. The employer may already have it, but at your interview you never know how many officials from the company you'll meet. Have extra copies handy.

Bring extra copies of your reference list, too. Encourage the employer to call your references. It will show them that you're confident in your abilities and in what people have to say about you.

Depending on the job, you may have some work-related documents, such as examples of an ad you created, samples of your writing, or even a portfolio, to show. Bring anything that may relate to the job you're seeking.

Bring a notebook and a pen. You may find it helpful to take some notes when the employer is talking, or you can jot down any questions that come to mind during the interview. Later, you can refer to your notes when it's time to ask questions.

A Good First Impression

There are many ways to make an impression. Walking into your interview with confidence, looking the employer in the eye, and smiling will go a long way. Here are some tips to help you positively adjust your behavior.

❑ **The handshake:** It's traditional in business meetings to shake hands, whether you're a man or a woman. There are many ways to shake a hand, and most are less-than-perfect versions of the handshake. Here's how to do it right. When you meet the person you're interviewing with, make eye contact and hold out your right hand. Grasp the other person's right hand firmly, but not too hard. A few small shakes and then release the hand, but keep the eye contact. A weak handshake or one that flails around for too long, on the other hand, may give the impression that you're nervous or even not trustworthy. If your hand is sweaty because you're nervous, try to dry it off before the interviewer sees.

❑ **Use your manners:** At the risk of sounding like your mother, I'll urge you to be on your best behavior and watch out for any bad habits you may have. Address the person you're meeting by name, using *Mr.* or *Ms.* and their last name, unless they tell you to call them by their first name. Sit up straight and don't slouch. Don't use profanity or slang. This will make you seem unprofessional. Show you have a command of the English language.

❑ **Have a positive attitude:** Your overall nature should come through when you're in an interview situation, talking about yourself. Make sure you sound optimistic and positive, and the employer will think of you as a can-do kind of person. A negative attitude gives off the vibes that you're someone who isn't willing to get the job done. If you're asked a hard question about your past experience or a lack of experience, spin an upbeat answer about your plans for the future and what you hope to accomplish with this job.

❑ **Sell yourself:** You need to be your own biggest advocate. If you don't tell the employer how wonderful you are, who else will? Now that doesn't mean you should boast and literally say, "I'm so great, hire me." Instead, focus on the positive qualities you're bringing to the table, and talk about what you can do for the employer and for the company. If you were hoping the interviewer would ask you about some of the successes on your résumé and they don't, create an opportunity in the conversation to talk about them.

Interview Tests

Depending on the type of job you're applying for, you might be asked to take a test during your interview. For a secretary's job, you may have to take a typing or word processing exam. Other jobs might require you to prove your writing skills by writing a memo or other interoffice communication.

If it's a writing test, take extra time to check your spelling and grammar. This is another opportunity to show off your command of English.

Employers may ask you to take other quizzes that test your knowledge. These may also backhandedly test your cultural awareness and your willingness to follow the rules.

For example, say you're applying for a job in a store. In your interview, you may be asked to take a written test to see how you would react to certain situations. Imagine the question:

> You're working in the store and your mom comes in to shop. You see her take some items and put them in her purse without paying. You:

- **a.** Don't say anything to her, but after she leaves the store, you tell management and pay for the items she took.
- **b.** Tell her to put the items back and send her home. You then buy the item for her and bring it home later.
- **c.** Call the police.

Of course your preference would be not to get your mother in trouble with the law. You'd rather pay for the items after she's left so you don't have to confront her or you'd tell her to put it back and then purchase the item for her anyway.

It's illegal to steal, period. The employer will want you to answer that you'd call the police. If you give that answer, someone is likely to ask you, "Would you really turn in your own mother?" They may be trying to trap you here, especially if they're not sure they want to hire you. Don't give them an opportunity to deny you a job based on your answer. In this case, you should then say, "The law is clear and if it's company policy to call the police on shoplifters, that's what I'd do."

Follow Up with a Note

After you leave your interview, go home and write a note to each of the people you interviewed with. It should be short and simple, thanking them for the opportunity to meet with them to discuss the job. It should go something like this:

Your Street
Your Town, State, Zip Code
Your e-mail address

Date

Mr./Ms. Name
Title
Company Name
Company Street
Company Town, State, Zip Code

Dear Mr./Ms. Name,

It was a pleasure to meet with you about the [name the type of job here] position at [name the company here]. The job seems to be a perfect match for my qualifications. [Say something specific about what the job requires and name a skill of yours that matches here.]

In addition to my high level of energy [or other quality here], I will bring to the job [name three different skills here]. My experience with [name your past experience here] will make a good fit with [name something particular you discussed during the interview here].

Once again, I appreciate the time you took to interview me. I'd be a great addition to your team, and I look forward to hearing from you about this position.

Sincerely,

Your Signature

Your Typed Name

Get a stamp and send the letter quickly, so the interviewer will receive it while the interview is fresh in his or her mind.

CHAPTER 7

Securing Your Victory

Congratulations! You've received a job offer. It's a very exciting time, and you should enjoy the feeling of accomplishment. But before you quickly ask your new employer, "When do I start?" you need to make sure you're getting the best possible deal.

You're going to be excited and nervous during this first phone call, and there's a good possibility you'll forget to ask many questions about the job, your responsibilities, your compensation, and your benefits.

When an employer calls you with a job offer, thank the employer and take notes on what he or she tells you about the position, the salary, and everything else that comes up during your conversation. Then ask the employer if you can have a day or so to think about it, and you'll call him back tomorrow.

Use this extra time wisely. You can use the time to think of all the questions you have about the job. Write a list of all your questions. The employer should be happy to answer your questions when you call him back.

Questions to Ask

Before you say, "I don't want to ask any questions. I need this job and I don't want to mess up this opportunity," slow down. Employers expect future employees to ask questions about a job and its perks. They even expect you to ask for more than they're offering. Of course you don't want to be viewed as a pest before you start the job, but you do want to make sure you're getting a reasonable deal for the job they're offering. Now, if you have a bad attitude when you're asking for information, the employer might think they're making a mistake by offering you the job. But if you have a professional manner, few employers will hold your questions against you.

THE SALARY

Before you start talking about pay with your future employer, you should have an idea of what others in similar positions at similar companies are earning. Salary.com's (www.salary.com) Salary Wizard is a tool you'll find on many job Web sites. It allows you to view salary ranges in your field based on job title and zip code. Plug in the information for the job you're trying to learn more about and you'll have an idea of what you should be paid.

Once you have an idea of the going rates, consider your experience, what skills you're bringing to the employer, and whether or not this job is a step up for you. If it is a step up, you might be willing to take the lower salary in exchange for the experience you'll get. If you already have significant experience in the area, the employer should be willing to pay a premium for an experienced worker. If you think you deserve more, the only way you'll get it is by asking. So you need to be prepared to negotiate.

Your salary conversation will probably start in one of two ways: either the employer will tell you a dollar figure he's willing to pay, or he may ask how much you want to be paid. You should treat both strategies differently.

A DOLLAR FIGURE

If the employer offers you a dollar figure, keep in mind what your research has told you about how much this type of position generally pays. If the offer number is in line, you're at a great starting point. That's right, a starting point. Employers expect employees to ask for more money. (It's generally easier to earn more over time if you negotiate a good price before you start the job. Asking for raises later can be harder.)

For example, imagine the employer starts with an offer of $30,000. You've done work in this field before and the job description exactly fits your qualifications. You know from your research that the job generally pays between $28,000 and $38,000, depending on experience. You have the experience the employer is looking for, so you're in a strong position. Consider a counteroffer, saying something such as, "The research I've done shows the salary range for this type of job is between $28,000 and $38,000, and I have four years of experience. I was hoping for a salary on the higher end of that range." Then wait for a response. The employer might immediately come back with a better number, or he may have to talk to his boss for authorization. That's good. On the other hand, he might tell you that that's all the company can pay for this job. In that case, you have to decide if the job is worth that salary to you.

HOW MUCH DO YOU WANT TO BE PAID?

The salary conversation can be harder if instead of making an offer, the employer ask you how much you want to be paid. Here you need to be patient, and part politician. You don't want to scare off or offend the employer by asking for a ridiculously high salary.

Instead, use your research again, and be ready to make a case for yourself. Take the same job as before, which has a salary range of $28,000 to $38,000 a year. If you have many years of experience, tell the employer something like, "I've been doing my current job for XYZ Company for four years and I've built up all the skills needed for someone in the position you're offering. My research shows this job generally pays between $28,000 and $38,000, with higher salaries for more experienced workers. I think I'm on the more experienced side."

Here, too, the employer may come back with an instantly sufficient offer or he may have to call you back. And if he says, "Sorry, we can't pay that much," you need to decide if the job is worth it.

NEGOTIATE FOR BENEFITS

If an employer can't or won't offer a higher salary, but you still really want the job, get creative. Tell him you'd take the job, but you can use three weeks of vacation instead of two. Or maybe the employer would be willing to pay your health care premiums for a certain time period. Or even give you a signing bonus, which is common in many sales jobs.

NOT ACCEPTING A JOB

If a new job offering isn't a step up from your current one, or if it's not going to give you enough of the things you need from a job, no one says you have to take it. If the offer isn't what you need or what you want, be prepared to walk away. (If you do, and the employer really wants you, he may pursue you even after you've turned him down.)

HEALTH AND DENTAL INSURANCE

Many, but not all, jobs offer health and/or dental insurance. This can be an enormous value-add to the total worth of a job offer. Health insurance means you'll be able to better afford the cost of care for your family should anyone get sick and need a doctor or, worse, end up with a hospital stay.

Some employer insurance plans are better than others. Don't expect the employer to be able to tell you if your favorite OB/GYN is listed on the company's health plan, but he should be able to tell you the basics. Some questions to ask:

- Do you offer health/dental insurance?
- What types of plans do you offer?
- What are the costs/premiums?
- Will my dependents/family be eligible for coverage?

Family health coverage, if you tried to buy an individual policy, could cost you hundreds of dollars a month. When you add this value to your salary compensation, it may make the job look even better.

RETIREMENT BENEFITS

Many companies offer retirement savings plans as a benefit to their workers. Plans vary, but the most common plans for public companies—401(k) plans—and for hospitals and schools—403(b) plans—

give workers an opportunity to save a portion of their salary to be set aside in an investment account for retirement. As an incentive, many companies also offer so-called matching funds. This means that for every dollar you save to the plan, the company adds a dollar to your account, up to a certain limit. There are also tax advantages to saving in these plans. (All the details of the plan will be explained to you during your orientation in the first few days on the job.)

If you're young, this especially might not seem like a big deal. But it is. You don't want to be working when you're ninety, if you can help it, and even if you're eligible for Social Security benefits from the U.S. government, they may not be enough to pay all your retirement bills.

Matching funds are essentially free money. Even if you leave the company someday, you'll get to keep the money. (Some companies say you must stay for a certain number of years to keep your matching funds, but the money you put in the account will always be yours.)

PAID PERSONAL DAYS, SICK DAYS, VACATION DAYS, AND HOLIDAYS

Many companies offer paid days off to employees, including a certain number of personal days or sick days a year, some vacation time, and paid holidays. Ask your employer how much vacation you're entitled to, and which holidays you can expect to have off. Depending on the type of company and the type of job you're considering, days off may vary. You should also ask what the company policies are regarding maternity and paternity leave.

DAY CARE ASSISTANCE

Employers are increasingly trying to help their employees balance their work and family lives. As such, many have instituted on-site day care facilities for the children of their workers. If you have kids who need day care, ask if the employer offers an on-site facility. If they don't, they may have a deal with a local day care center that offers subsidized day care for employees of your company. (That means you pay a portion of the fee and your company pays a portion.) Those benefits may add up, too.

PERFORMANCE REVIEWS AND RAISES

After you've been working for a few months, your employer is likely to plan a review, during which you sit down with your supervisor and discuss how you've done at the company so far. At this time, the employer may offer you a raise. Ask your future employer when you can expect a performance review, what it will entail, and whether or not raises should be expected after a positive review. You should also ask, after your first review, how often raises are considered.

HOW OFTEN WILL I BE PAID?

Companies vary in how frequently they pay their employees. Some give paychecks every week, some every two weeks, and some give paychecks only once a month. Others may pay on a delay; for example, you may not get paid the first week, and in the second week you'll get the first week's paycheck, and so on. After you leave the job, you'll still have one week's pay coming to you. Adjusting to a new pay schedule may be a challenge for you, but you can do it, as long as you plan ahead. That's why you should know the pay schedule before you accept a job.

WHAT ARE ALL YOUR BENEFITS WORTH?

After you've asked about all the benefits that come with your new job, take a moment to put a dollar figure to it so you can see what the total compensation is worth. Check out the Benefits Calculator at Salary. com for some help in making your calculations.

Your First Day on the Job

Start with your best foot forward. Just as you planned to get to your interview on time, revisit that plan for your first day. Make sure you dress appropriately, and remember that you're better off being too conservative until you get a feel for how this new place of employment operates.

When you arrive at your new job, your employer, or your new supervisor, will probably show you around the office. You should learn where you can leave your personal items (perhaps a desk that will be assigned to you or a locker), you'll learn where to find the bathrooms, the lunchroom or break room, and other places not directly related to performing your job. (A coworker will probably be assigned to train you on specific tasks.)

Sometime during your first day or your first week, you'll be asked to fill out a bunch of paperwork. Here's what you should expect, and note the identification and other information you should bring from home.

TAX PAPERWORK

One of the first batches of paperwork you'll be asked to complete will be tax forms, more specifically, a W-4 form. All employees in the United States pay taxes, and how you fill out these forms determines how much money will be taken out of your paycheck each week for taxes. (You can find a copy of the W-4 in Appendix B of this book.)

One of the most confusing parts of the W-4 is when you're asked how many dependents you have, between zero and four. The more dependents you have, the less money will be taken out of your paycheck for taxes. But if you're not careful here, and not enough money is taken out from your paycheck for taxes each paycheck, when you file your taxes on April 15, you'll likely owe the government more money.

If you have two children, you may choose to claim two dependents. If you're married with two children, and your spouse relies on your income and doesn't work, you may want to claim three dependents. If your spouse does work, you may only want to claim two dependents. You also have the option of counting yourself as a dependent, too.

If you're not sure how many dependents to claim, consider calling your tax preparer for some advice. Or, err on the side of caution and claim yourself and your number of children. You may have slightly less in your paycheck, but you probably won't owe additional tax monies on April 15.

Keep in mind that you may also be asked to fill out a separate state tax form, depending on the state in which you're working.

WORKING IN THE UNITED STATES

After tax forms, you'll be asked to provide paperwork to prove that you're eligible to work in the United States. Employers are required by law to make sure their employees, whether they're born in the United States or not, have authority to work in the United States. For this, they will ask you to fill out a form called I-9, the Employment Eligibility Verification Form. Try to have all the necessary authorization documents with you. You will need:

- Permanent Resident Card (Also known as Resident Alien Card, Alien Registration Receipt Card, and Form I-551. Note: Although an expired card does not qualify, an individual cannot be denied employment because his or her card is going to expire soon.)
- Two forms of identification, such as:
  - Driver's license with a photo ID
  - Other photo ID issued by a federal, state, or local government office
  - Birth certificate
  - Passport
  - Social Security card

The I-9 Form, found in Appendix C of this book, lists acceptable documents for proof of work eligibility.

DIRECT DEPOSIT

You may be offered the option of having your paycheck directly deposited into your bank account. Direct deposit means that your employer will send your paycheck directly to your bank, and the money will be available in your checking account on payday. You don't have to use direct deposit, but it has advantages. You won't have to visit the bank to make deposits, and your money will be available immediately.

If you want direct deposit, also called automatic deposit, bring a voided blank check with you (simply a check with the word VOID handwritten across it so no one can use it), your bank account number (found on your statements or your checks), your bank's name, address, phone number, and routing number. The routing number is simply the code that financial institutions use to make sure money is delivered to the correct banks. Your routing number can be found on your checks, preprinted on the lower left-hand corner. If you're not sure, bring a check with you and the human resources or benefits manager at your company can help.

You can find a sample direct deposit form in Appendix D of this book.

LIFE INSURANCE BENEFITS

If your employer offers life insurance benefits (where your company pays for you to have a life insurance policy at low or no cost), you'll need to bring information about your beneficiaries. Your beneficiaries might be your spouse, your children, your siblings, or your parents—the person or people you want to receive money from the insurance company should you die. You'll have to provide the names and addresses of your beneficiaries.

HEALTH INSURANCE BENEFITS

If your company offers health insurance, you'll have to fill out some paperwork to sign up. If the plan provides coverage for family members, you'll also have to give their names and information, such as age and relationship to you. If you're lucky, you may have the opportunity to choose among a few different plans. They're likely to have different benefits and different levels of cost. Because plans can vary so much, ask your benefits counselor to explain the differences.

RETIREMENT BENEFITS

Retirement benefits, such as a 401(k) or 403(b) plan, are your chance to put money away for the future. If your company offers a plan, take advantage. You'll be asked to sign up, decide what percentage of your salary you want to contribute, and choose what kinds of investments you want your money to be put in.

Here are the basics on how these plans work.

❑ They allow you to put away pretax money for retirement—with most plans you can't access the money without penalty until you reach age 59½. Pretax money is money before taxes are taken out. For example, if you have a $30,000 salary and you contribute $3,000 a year to your

401(k) plan, your taxable income for the year is only $27,000. So not only are you saving for your future, you're being taxed less today.

- Another advantage is that the money you save grows tax-deferred. That means you won't have to pay taxes on the account's earnings. Say you contribute $3,000 in the first year to your account, and the investments in the account earned $500. You don't have to pay taxes on that $500 until you withdraw it at retirement. If you invested the same $3,000 in a nonemployer account, such as at a bank, you'd have to pay taxes on that $500 profit.

- Most plans allow you to choose from several investment options. They generally include mutual funds, which are investments that buy many stocks and bonds. When you own a mutual fund, you're able to own small pieces of all those stocks and bonds. Over time, history shows the stock market has grown in value. Some days are up, some days are down, but averaged over the long term, stocks earn money. If you're young and very far away from retirement, consider investing in some of the more aggressive investments in your 401(k). If you're an older worker, think about staying more conservative because you'll theoretically be needing the money sooner, if you decide to retire. Your benefits counselor should be able to explain the different options available to you.

- How much should you contribute to the plan? That's a very individual decision. Of course you need money to live today, but if you want to plan for the future, you should, and you must, take advantage of your employer's retirement plan. It is very important that even if it's a small amount, as little as $20 a paycheck, you put something away. Most financial planners say that, at the very least, you should contribute enough to get as much of the employer's match as you can.

Enjoy Your Success

So now you've made it. You're ready to start a great new job, with exciting prospects for the future. Remember how hard you've worked to get this far, and show your new employer he made the right decision in selecting you. Enjoy it!

Appendix A

*List of Common Action Words to Use in
Résumés and Cover Letters*

Achieve	Establish	Preside
Administer	Evaluate	Program
Advise	Execute	Promote
Analyze	Expand	Recommend
Apply	Formulate	Reduce
Arrange	Gather	Regulate
Bolster	Generate	Reorganize
Boost	Guide	Research
Budget	Implement	Review
Calculate	Improve	Revise
Classify	Initiate	Schedule
Communicate	Institute	Select
Complete	Introduce	Solve
Compute	Invent	Spearhead
Coordinate	Issue	Strengthen
Conceptualize	Launch	Supervise
Create	Lead	Systematize
Critique	Lobby	Teach
Delegate	Manage	Test
Deliver	Negotiate	Trace
Design	Operate	Train
Determine	Organize	Transform
Develop	Overhaul	Trim
Devise	Plan	Update
Direct	Prepare	Utilize
Enlarge	Present	Write

Appendix B

W-4 Form

Form W-4 (2006)

Purpose. Complete Form W-4 so that your employer can withhold the correct federal income tax from your pay. Because your tax situation may change, you may want to refigure your withholding each year.

Exemption from withholding. If you are exempt, complete only lines 1, 2, 3, 4, and 7 and sign the form to validate it. Your exemption for 2006 expires February 16, 2007. See Pub. 505, Tax Withholding and Estimated Tax.

Note. You cannot claim exemption from withholding if (a) your income exceeds $850 and includes more than $300 of unearned income (for example, interest and dividends) and (b) another person can claim you as a dependent on their tax return.

Basic instructions. If you are not exempt, complete the **Personal Allowances Worksheet** below. The worksheets on page 2 adjust your withholding allowances based on itemized deductions, certain credits, adjustments to income, or two-

earner/two-job situations. Complete all worksheets that apply. However, you may claim fewer (or zero) allowances.

Head of household. Generally, you may claim head of household filing status on your tax return only if you are unmarried and pay more than 50% of the costs of keeping up a home for yourself and your dependent(s) or other qualifying individuals. See line E below.

Tax credits. You can take projected tax credits into account in figuring your allowable number of withholding allowances. Credits for child or dependent care expenses and the child tax credit may be claimed using the **Personal Allowances Worksheet** below. See Pub. 919, How Do I Adjust My Tax Withholding, for information on converting your other credits into withholding allowances.

Nonwage income. If you have a large amount of nonwage income, such as interest or dividends, consider making estimated tax payments using Form 1040-ES, Estimated Tax for Individuals. Otherwise, you may owe additional tax.

Two earners/two jobs. If you have a working spouse or more than one job, figure the total number of allowances you are entitled to claim on all jobs using worksheets from only one Form W-4. Your withholding usually will be most accurate when all allowances are claimed on the Form W-4 for the highest paying job and zero allowances are claimed on the others.

Nonresident alien. If you are a nonresident alien, see the Instructions for Form 8233 before completing this Form W-4.

Check your withholding. After your Form W-4 takes effect, use Pub. 919 to see how the dollar amount you are having withheld compares to your projected total tax for 2006. See Pub. 919, especially if your earnings exceed $130,000 (Single) or $180,000 (Married).

Recent name change? If your name on line 1 differs from that shown on your social security card, call 1-800-772-1213 to initiate a name change and obtain a social security card showing your correct name.

Personal Allowances Worksheet (Keep for your records.)

A   Enter "1" for **yourself** if no one else can claim you as a dependent . . . . **A** ____

B   Enter "1" if: {   • You are single and have only one job; or
             • You are married, have only one job, and your spouse does not work; or
             • Your wages from a second job or your spouse's wages (or the total of both) are $1,000 or less.   }   **B** ____

C   Enter "1" for your **spouse.** But, you may choose to enter "-0-" if you are married and have either a working spouse or more than one job. (Entering "-0-" may help you avoid having too little tax withheld.) . . . . . **C** ____

D   Enter number of **dependents** (other than your spouse or yourself) you will claim on your tax return . . . **D** ____

E   Enter "1" if you will file as **head of household** on your tax return (see conditions under **Head of household** above) . **E** ____

F   Enter "1" if you have at least $1,500 of **child or dependent care expenses** for which you plan to claim a credit . **F** ____

(**Note.** Do **not** include child support payments. See **Pub. 503,** Child and Dependent Care Expenses, for details.)

G   **Child Tax Credit** (including additional child tax credit):
   • If your total income will be less than $55,000 ($82,000 if married), enter "2" for each eligible child.
   • If your total income will be between $55,000 and $84,000 ($82,000 and $119,000 if married), enter "1" for each eligible child plus "1" **additional** if you have four or more eligible children.   . . . . **G** ____

H Add lines A through G and enter total here. (**Note.** This may be different from the number of exemptions you claim on your tax return.) ▶ **H** _____

For accuracy, complete all worksheets that apply. {
- If you plan to **itemize or claim adjustments to income** and want to reduce your withholding, see the **Deductions and Adjustments Worksheet** on page 2.
- If you have **more than one job** or are **married** and you and your spouse **both work** and the combined earnings from all jobs exceed $35,000 ($25,000 if married) see the **Two-Earner/Two-Job Worksheet** on page 2 to avoid having too little tax withheld.
- If **neither** of the above situations applies, **stop here** and enter the number from line H on line 5 of Form W-4 below.
}

- - - - - - - - - Cut here and give Form W-4 to your employer. Keep the top part for your records. - - - - - - - - -

Form **W-4**	**Employee's Withholding Allowance Certificate**	OMB No. 1545-0074
Department of the Treasury Internal Revenue Service	▶ Whether you are entitled to claim a certain number of allowances or exemption from withholding is subject to review by the IRS. Your employer may be required to **send a copy of this form to the IRS.**	**2006**

1 Type or print your first name and middle initial.	Last name		**2** Your social security number

Home address (number and street or rural route)	**3** ☐ Single ☐ Married ☐ Married, but withhold at higher Single rate. **Note.** If married, but legally separated, or spouse is a nonresident alien, check the "Single" box.
City or town, state, and ZIP code	**4** If your last name differs from that shown on your social security card, check here. **You must call 1-800-772-1213 for a new card.** ▶ ☐

5 Total number of allowances you are claiming (from line **H** above **or** from the applicable worksheet on page 2)			**5**
6 Additional amount, if any, you want withheld from each paycheck			**6** $
7 I claim exemption from withholding for 2006, and I certify that I meet **both** of the following conditions for exemption.			
• Last year I had a right to a refund of **all** federal income tax withheld because I had **no** tax liability **and**			
• This year I expect a refund of **all** federal income tax withheld because I expect to have **no** tax liability.			
If you meet both conditions, write "Exempt" here . . . . ▶		**7**	

Under penalties of perjury, I declare that I have examined this certificate and to the best of my knowledge and belief, it is true, correct, and complete.

Employee's signature
(Form is not valid
unless you sign it.) ▶ _____ **Date** ▶ _____

8 Employer's name and address (Employer: Complete lines 8 and 10 only if sending to the IRS.)	**9** Office code (optional)	**10** Employer identification number (EIN)

For Privacy Act and Paperwork Reduction Act Notice, see page 2.   Cat. No. 10220Q   Form **W-4** (2006)

Form W-4 (2006)   Page **2**

Deductions and Adjustments Worksheet

Note. Use this worksheet *only* if you plan to itemize deductions, claim certain credits, or claim adjustments to income on your 2006 tax return.

1 Enter an estimate of your 2006 itemized deductions. These include qualifying home mortgage interest, charitable contributions, state and local taxes, medical expenses in excess of 7.5% of your income, and miscellaneous deductions. (For 2006, you may have to reduce your itemized deductions if your income is over $150,500 ($75,250 if married filing separately). See *Worksheet 3* in Pub. 919 for details.) . . . . . . **1** $

2 Enter: { $10,300 if married filing jointly or qualifying widow(er) } . . . . **2** $
              { $ 7,550 if head of household }
              { $ 5,150 if single or married filing separately }

3 **Subtract** line 2 from line 1. If line 2 is greater than line 1, enter "-0-" . . . . **3** $

4 Enter an estimate of your 2006 adjustments to income, including alimony, deductible IRA contributions, and student loan interest **4** $

5 **Add** lines 3 and 4 and enter the total. (Include any amount for credits from *Worksheet 7* in Pub. 919) . . **5** $

6 Enter an estimate of your 2006 nonwage income (such as dividends or interest) . . . . **6** $

7 **Subtract** line 6 from line 5. Enter the result, but not less than "-0-" . . . . **7** $

8 **Divide** the amount on line 7 by $3,300 and enter the result here. Drop any fraction **8**

9 Enter the number from the **Personal Allowances Worksheet,** line H, page 1 . . . . **9**

10 **Add** lines 8 and 9 and enter the total here. If you plan to use the **Two-Earner/Two-Job Worksheet,** also enter this total on line 1 below. Otherwise, **stop here** and enter this total on Form W-4, line 5, page 1 . . **10**

Two-Earner/Two-Job Worksheet (See *Two earners/two jobs* on page 1.)

Note. Use this worksheet *only* if the instructions under line H on page 1 direct you here.

1 Enter the number from line H, page 1 (or from line 10 above if you used the **Deductions and Adjustments Worksheet**) **1**

2 Find the number in **Table 1** below that applies to the **LOWEST** paying job and enter it here . . . **2**

3 If line 1 is **more than or equal to** line 2, subtract line 2 from line 1. Enter the result here (if zero, enter "-0-") and on Form W-4, line 5, page 1. **Do not** use the rest of this worksheet **3**

Note. If line 1 is *less than* line 2, enter "-0-" on Form W-4, line 5, page 1. Complete lines 4-9 below to calculate the additional withholding amount necessary to avoid a year-end tax bill.

4 Enter the number from line 2 of this worksheet **4**

5 Enter the number from line 1 of this worksheet **5**

6 **Subtract** line 5 from line 4 . . . . **6**

7 Find the amount in **Table 2** below that applies to the **HIGHEST** paying job and enter it here . . . **7** $

8 **Multiply** line 7 by line 6 and enter the result here. This is the additional annual withholding needed . **8** $

9   Divide line 8 by the number of pay periods remaining in 2006. For example, divide by 26 if you are paid every two weeks and you complete this form in December 2005. Enter the result here and on Form W-4, line 6, page 1. This is the additional amount to be withheld from each paycheck . . . . . .   **9** $

Table 1: Two-Earner/Two-Job Worksheet

Married Filing Jointly					All Others	
If wages from **HIGHEST** paying job are—	AND, wages from **LOWEST** paying job are—	Enter on line 2 above	If wages from **HIGHEST** paying job are—	AND, wages from **LOWEST** paying job are—	If wages from **LOWEST** paying job are—	Enter on line 2 above
$0 - $42,000	$0 - $4,500	0	$42,001 and over	32,001 - 38,000	$0 - $6,000	0
	4,501 - 9,000	1		38,001 - 46,000	6,001 - 12,000	1
	9,001 - 18,000	2		46,001 - 55,000	12,001 - 19,000	2
	18,001 and over	3		55,001 - 60,000	19,001 - 26,000	3
				60,001 - 65,000	26,001 - 35,000	4
$42,001 and over	$0 - $4,500	0		65,001 - 75,000	35,001 - 50,000	5
	4,501 - 9,000	1		75,001 - 95,000	50,001 - 65,000	6
	9,001 - 18,000	2		95,001 - 105,000	65,001 - 80,000	7
	18,001 - 22,000	3		105,001 - 120,000	80,001 - 90,000	8
	22,001 - 26,000	4		120,001 and over	90,001 - 120,000	9
	26,001 - 32,000	5			120,001 and over	10

Enter on line 2 above (for $42,001 and over column): 6, 7, 8, 9, 10, 11, 12, 13, 14, 15

Table 2: Two-Earner/Two-Job Worksheet

Married Filing Jointly		All Others	
If wages from **HIGHEST** paying job are—	Enter on line 7 above	If wages from **HIGHEST** paying job are—	Enter on line 7 above
$0 - $60,000	$500	$0 - $30,000	$500
60,001 - 115,000	830	30,001 - 75,000	830
115,001 - 165,000	920	75,001 - 145,000	920
165,001 - 290,000	1,090	145,001 - 330,000	1,090
290,001 and over	1,160	330,001 and over	1,160

Privacy Act and Paperwork Reduction Act Notice. We ask for the information on this form to carry out the Internal Revenue laws of the United States. The Internal Revenue Code requires this information under sections 3402(f)(2)(A) and 6109 and their regulations. Failure to provide a properly completed form will result in your being treated as a single person who claims no withholding allowances; providing fraudulent information may also subject you to penalties. Routine uses of this information include giving it to the Department of Justice for civil and criminal litigation, to cities, states, and the District of Columbia for use in administering their tax laws, and using it in the National Directory of New Hires. We may also disclose this information to other countries under a tax treaty, to federal and state agencies to enforce federal nontax criminal laws, or to federal law enforcement and intelligence agencies to combat terrorism.

You are not required to provide the information requested on a form that is subject to the Paperwork Reduction Act unless the form displays a valid OMB control number. Books or records relating to a form or its instructions must be retained as long as their contents may become material in the administration of any Internal Revenue law. Generally, tax returns and return information are confidential, as required by Code section 6103.

The average time and expenses required to complete and file this form will vary depending on individual circumstances. For estimated averages, see the instructions for your income tax return.

If you have suggestions for making this form simpler, we would be happy to hear from you. See the instructions for your income tax return.

Appendix C

Employment Eligibility Forms

Department of Homeland Security
U.S. Citizenship and Immigration Services

OMB No. 1615-0047; Expires 03/31/07

Employment Eligibility Verification

INSTRUCTIONS

PLEASE READ ALL INSTRUCTIONS CAREFULLY BEFORE COMPLETING THIS FORM.

Anti-Discrimination Notice. It is illegal to discriminate against any individual (other than an alien not authorized to work in the U.S.) in hiring, discharging, or recruiting or referring for a fee because of that individual's national origin or citizenship status. It is illegal to discriminate against work eligible individuals. Employers **CANNOT** specify which document(s) they will accept from an employee. The refusal to hire an individual because of a future expiration date may also constitute illegal discrimination.

Section 1- Employee. All employees, citizens and noncitizens, hired after November 6, 1986, must complete Section 1 of this form at the time of hire, which is the actual beginning of employment. **The employer is responsible for ensuring that Section 1 is timely and properly completed.**

Preparer/Translator Certification. The Preparer/Translator Certification must be completed if Section 1 is prepared by a person other than the employee. A preparer/translator may be used only when the employee is unable to complete Section 1 on his/her own. However, the employee must still sign Section 1 personally.

Section 2 - Employer. For the purpose of completing this form, the term "employer" includes those recruiters and referrers for a fee who are agricultural associations, agricultural employers or farm labor contractors.

Employers must complete Section 2 by examining evidence of identity and employment eligibility within three (3) business days of the date employment begins. If employees are authorized to work, but are unable to present the required document(s) within three business days, they must present a receipt for the application of the document(s) within three business days and the actual document(s)

- examine any document that reflects that the employee is authorized to work in the U.S. (see List A or C),

- record the document title, document number and expiration date (if any) in Block C, and

- complete the signature block.

Photocopying and Retaining Form I-9. A blank I-9 may be reproduced, provided both sides are copied. The Instructions must be available to all employees completing this form. Employers must retain completed I-9s for three (3) years after the date of hire or one (1) year after the date employment ends, whichever is later.

For more detailed information, you may refer to the Department of Homeland Security (DHS) Handbook for Employers (Form M-274). You may obtain the handbook at your local U.S. Citizenship and Immigration Services (USCIS) office.

Privacy Act Notice. The authority for collecting this information is the Immigration Reform and Control Act of 1986, Pub. L. 99-603 (8 USC 1324a).

This information is for employers to verify the eligibility of individuals for employment to preclude the unlawful hiring, or recruiting or

within ninety (90) days. However, if employers hire individuals for a duration of less than three business days, **Section 2** must be completed at the time employment begins. **Employers must record: 1)** document title; **2)** issuing authority; **3)** document number, **4)** expiration date, if any; and **5)** the date employment begins.
Employers must sign and date the certification. Employees must present original documents. Employers may, but are not required to, photocopy the document(s) presented. These photocopies may only be used for the verification process and must be retained with the I-9. **However, employers are still responsible for completing the I-9.**

Section 3 - Updating and Reverification.
Employers must complete Section 3 when updating and/or reverifying the I-9. Employers must reverify employment eligibility of their employees on or before the expiration date recorded in Section 1. Employers **CANNOT** specify which document(s) they will accept from an employee.

- If an employee's name has changed at the time this form is being updated/reverified, complete Block A.

- If an employee is rehired within three (3) years of the date this form was originally completed and the employee is still eligible to be employed on the same basis as previously indicated on this form (updating), complete Block B and the signature block.

- If an employee is rehired within three (3) years of the date this form was originally completed and the employee's work authorization has expired **or** if a current employee's work authorization is about to expire (reverification), complete Block B and:

referring for a fee, of aliens who are not authorized to work in the United States.

This information will be used by employers as a record of their basis for determining eligibility of an employee to work in the United States. The form will be kept by the employer and made available for inspection by officials of the U.S. Immigration and Customs Enforcement, Department of Labor and Office of Special Counsel for Immigration Related Unfair Employment Practices.

Submission of the information required in this form is voluntary. However, an individual may not begin employment unless this form is completed, since employers are subject to civil or criminal penalties if they do not comply with the Immigration Reform and Control Act of 1986.

Reporting Burden. We try to create forms and instructions that are accurate, can be easily understood and which impose the least possible burden on you to provide us with information. Often this is difficult because some immigration laws are very complex. Accordingly, the reporting burden for this collection of information is computed as follows: **1)** learning about this form, 5 minutes; **2)** completing the form, 5 minutes; and **3)** assembling and filing (recordkeeping) the form, 5 minutes, for an average of 15 minutes per response. If you have comments regarding the accuracy of this burden estimate, or suggestions for making this form simpler, you can write to U.S. Citizenship and Immigration Services. Regulatory Management Division, 111 Massachusetts Avenue, N.W., Washington, DC 20529. OMB No. 1615-0047.

NOTE: This is the 1991 edition of the Form I-9 that has been rebranded with a current printing date to reflect the recent transition from the INS to DHS and its components.

Form I-9 (Rev. 05/31/05)Y

**EMPLOYERS MUST RETAIN COMPLETED FORM I-9
PLEASE DO NOT MAIL COMPLETED FORM I-9 TO ICE OR USCIS**

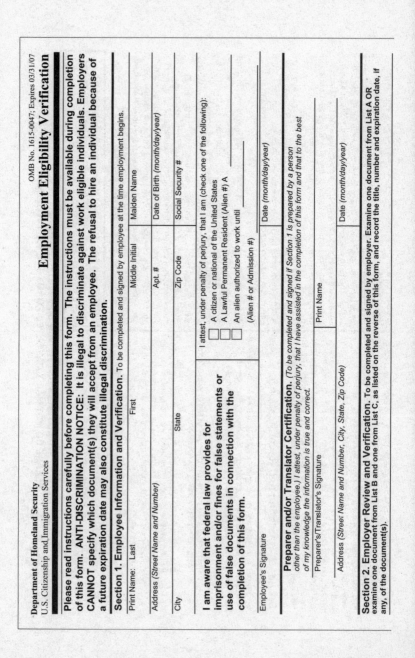

Department of Homeland Security
U.S. Citizenship and Immigration Services

OMB No. 1615-0047; Expires 03/31/07

Employment Eligibility Verification

Please read instructions carefully before completing this form. The instructions must be available during completion of this form. **ANTI-DISCRIMINATION NOTICE: It is illegal to discriminate against work eligible individuals. Employers CANNOT specify which document(s) they will accept from an employee. The refusal to hire an individual because of a future expiration date may also constitute illegal discrimination.**

Section 1. Employee Information and Verification. To be completed and signed by employee at the time employment begins.

Print Name: Last	First	Middle Initial	Maiden Name

Address *(Street Name and Number)*		Apt. #	Date of Birth *(month/day/year)*

City	State	Zip Code	Social Security #

I am aware that federal law provides for imprisonment and/or fines for false statements or use of false documents in connection with the completion of this form.

I attest, under penalty of perjury, that I am (check one of the following):

☐ A citizen or national of the United States
☐ A Lawful Permanent Resident (Alien #) A _____
☐ An alien authorized to work until _____
(Alien # or Admission #)

Employee's Signature	Date *(month/day/year)*

Preparer and/or Translator Certification. *(To be completed and signed if Section 1 is prepared by a person other than the employee.) I attest, under penalty of perjury, that I have assisted in the completion of this form and that to the best of my knowledge the information is true and correct.*

Preparer's/Translator's Signature	Print Name

Address *(Street Name and Number, City, State, Zip Code)*	Date *(month/day/year)*

Section 2. Employer Review and Verification. To be completed and signed by employer. Examine one document from List A OR examine one document from List B and one from List C, as listed on the reverse of this form, and record the title, number and expiration date, if any, of the document(s).

List A	OR	List B	AND	List C

Document title: _____

Issuing authority: _____

Document #: _____

Expiration Date (if any): _____

Document #: _____

Expiration Date (if any): _____

CERTIFICATION - I attest, under penalty of perjury, that I have examined the document(s) presented by the above-named employee, that the above-listed document(s) appear to be genuine and to relate to the employee named, that the employee began employment on (month/day/year) _____ **and that to the best of my knowledge the employee is eligible to work in the United States. (State employment agencies may omit the date the employee began employment.)**

Signature of Employer or Authorized Representative	Print Name	Title

Business or Organization Name	Address (Street Name and Number, City, State, Zip Code)	Date (month/day/year)

Section 3. Updating and Reverification. To be completed and signed by employer.

A. New Name (if applicable) _____   B. Date of Rehire (month/day/year) (if applicable) _____

C. If employee's previous grant of work authorization has expired, provide the information below for the document that establishes current employment eligibility.   Document Title: _____ Document #: _____ Expiration Date (if any): _____

I attest, under penalty of perjury, that to the best of my knowledge, this employee is eligible to work in the United States, and if the employee presented document(s), the document(s) I have examined appear to be genuine and to relate to the individual.

Signature of Employer or Authorized Representative		Date (month/day/year)

NOTE: This is the 1991 edition of the Form I-9 that has been rebranded with a current printing date to reflect the recent transition from the INS to DHS and its components.

Form I-9 (Rev. 05/31/05)Y Page 2

LISTS OF ACCEPTABLE DOCUMENTS

LIST A		LIST B		LIST C
Documents that Establish Both Identity and Employment Eligibility	OR	Documents that Establish Identity	AND	Documents that Establish Employment Eligibility

LIST A — Documents that Establish Both Identity and Employment Eligibility

1. U.S. Passport (unexpired or expired)

2. Certificate of U.S. Citizenship *(Form N-560 or N-561)*

3. Certificate of Naturalization *(Form N-550 or N-570)*

4. Unexpired foreign passport, with *I-551 stamp or attached Form I-94* indicating unexpired employment authorization

5. Permanent Resident Card or Alien Registration Receipt Card with photograph *(Form I-151 or I-551)*

LIST B — Documents that Establish Identity

1. Driver's license or ID card issued by a state or outlying possession of the United States provided it contains a photograph or information such as name, date of birth, gender, height, eye color and address

2. ID card issued by federal, state or local government agencies or entities, provided it contains a photograph or information such as name, date of birth, gender, height, eye color and address

3. School ID card with a photograph

4. Voter's registration card

5. U.S. Military card or draft record

LIST C — Documents that Establish Employment Eligibility

1. U.S. social security card issued by the Social Security Administration *(other than a card stating it is not valid for employment)*

2. Certification of Birth Abroad issued by the Department of State *(Form FS-545 or Form DS-1350)*

3. Original or certified copy of a birth certificate issued by a state, county, municipal authority or outlying possession of the United States bearing an official seal

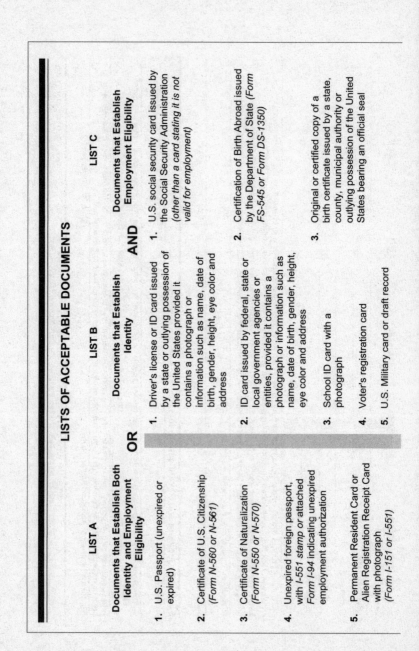

6. Unexpired Temporary Resident Card (*Form I-688*)

7. Unexpired Employment Authorization Card (*Form I-688A*)

8. Unexpired Reentry Permit (*Form I-327*)

9. Unexpired Refugee Travel Document (*Form I-571*)

10. Unexpired Employment Authorization Document issued by DHS that contains a photograph (*Form I-688B*)

6. Military dependent's ID card

7. U.S. Coast Guard Merchant Mariner Card

8. Native American tribal document

9. Driver's license issued by a Canadian government authority

For persons under age 18 who are unable to present a document listed above:

10. School record or report card

11. Clinic, doctor or hospital record

12. Day-care or nursery school record

4. Native American tribal document

5. U.S. Citizen ID Card (*Form I-197*)

6. ID Card for use of Resident Citizen in the United States (*Form I-179*)

7. Unexpired employment authorization document issued by DHS (*other than those listed under List A*)

Illustrations of many of these documents appear in Part 8 of the Handbook for Employers (M-274)

Appendix D

Direct Deposit Form

Fermilab

Fermi National Accelerator Laboratory
P.O. Box • 500 • Batavia, Illinois • 60510

DIRECT DEPOSIT

PLEASE INDICATE: CHANGE: _____   NEW ENROLLEE: _____

IMPORTANT: By providing the information below, all prior authorizations are voided

Employee Pay Group
WEEKLY   MONTHLY
(Circle One)

Department Name/Address (Optional)

Effective Date

Employee ID

Employee Name

1) Financial Institution (Bank Routing No.)

Account Number

☐ Savings Account
☐ Checking Account

ACCT AMT/PCT

2) Financial Institution (Bank Routing No.)

Account Number

☐ Savings Account
☐ Checking Account

ACCT AMT/PCT

3) Financial Institution (Bank Routing No.)

Account Number

☐ Savings Account
☐ Checking Account

ACCT AMT/PCT

3) Argonne Credit Union (Bank Routing No.)

Account Number

☐ Savings Account
☐ Checking Account

ACCT AMT/PCT *

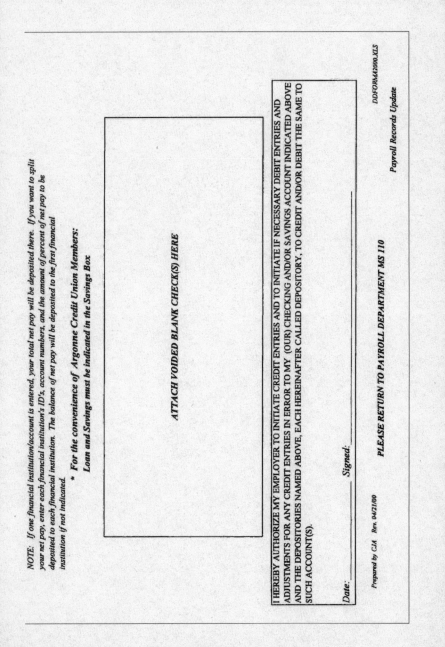

NOTE: If one financial institution/account is entered, your total net pay will be deposited there. If you want to split your net pay, enter each financial institution's ID's, account numbers, and the amount of percent of net pay to be deposited to each financial institution. The balance of net pay will be deposited to the first financial institution if not indicated.

* For the convenience of Argonne Credit Union Members:
  Loan and Savings must be indicated in the Savings Box

ATTACH VOIDED BLANK CHECK(S) HERE

I HEREBY AUTHORIZE MY EMPLOYER TO INITIATE CREDIT ENTRIES AND TO INITIATE IF NECESSARY DEBIT ENTRIES AND ADJUSTMENTS FOR ANY CREDIT ENTRIES IN ERROR TO MY (OUR) CHECKING AND/OR SAVINGS ACCOUNT INDICATED ABOVE AND THE DEPOSITORIES NAMED ABOVE, EACH HEREINAFTER CALLED DEPOSITORY, TO CREDIT AND/OR DEBIT THE SAME TO SUCH ACCOUNT(S).

Date: _____ Signed: _____

Prepared by CJA Rev. 04/21/00 PLEASE RETURN TO PAYROLL DEPARTMENT MS 110

DDFORM2000.XLS

Payroll Records Update

About the Authors

The Reverend Luis Cortés Jr. is the president and CEO of Esperanza USA, the largest Hispanic faith-based community development corporation in the country. In January 2005, he was featured as one of *Time* magazine's "25 Most Influential Evangelicals."

Karin Price Mueller is an award-winning writer and television producer. She's a personal finance columnist for *The Star-Ledger*, New Jersey's largest newspaper, and a frequent contributor to magazines, including *Ladies' Home Journal*. Mueller is the author of *Online Money Management* (Microsoft Press, 2001) and collaborated on *How to Fix Your Credit*, by the Reverend Luis Cortés Jr. She started her career in television, as a producer for CNBC and CNNfn. She lives in New Jersey with her husband, three kids, one dog, and two leopard geckos.